DAYS OF LEAD

MOSHE RASHKES

DAYS OF LEAD

DEFYING DEATH DURING ISRAEL'S WAR OF INDEPENDENCE

FOREWORD BY SENATOR (RET.) MAX CLELAND
PREFACE BY ARIK RASHKES

APOLLO
PUBLISHERS

Days of Lead

Defying Death During Israel's War of Independence

Copyright © 2021 by Arik Rashkes.
First printed in hardcover in 2018.

Apollo Publishers books may be purchased for educational, business, or sales promotional use. Special editions may be made available upon request. For details, contact Apollo Publishers at info@apollopublishers.com.

Visit our website at www.apollopublishers.com.

Published in compliance with California's Proposition 65.
Library of Congress Control Number: 2017962379

Cover design by Rain Saukas.
Cover image copyright © National Photo Collection, Israel.

Print ISBN: 978-1-948062-91-6
Ebook ISBN: 978-1-948062-09-1

Printed in the United States of America.

In memory of my parents,
Golda and Ariye Leib.

CONTENTS

FOREWORD

BY SENATOR (RET.) MAX CLELAND

I t was a great honor for me to be asked to pen an introduction to this important book, which received excellent reviews and was printed in Israel in nine editions.

The greatness of this book is to be found in its atmosphere, which enables readers to identify deeply with the author, as if they themselves were on the battlefield, experiencing the terrible pain and sensation of loss.

As a combatant in 1968, I lost both legs and an arm in the Vietnam War. The US government awarded me Bronze and Silver Stars for valorous actions in combat. Following my rehabilitation, I felt the need to serve the American public, first as secretary of state for Georgia, and later as a US senator.

So why am I writing about this particular book? Not just because Moshe Rashkes is a close personal friend, or because the book's subject matter is close to my heart and my difficult life experiences. It seems that every meeting with the Angel of Death, and every escape from his clutches, lead to enormous changes in the soul of an individual. For most, these changes result in a desire to make things better for humanity and, in wartime, to help one's fellow combatants.

Moshe followed the same path as I did. Even while hospitalized, following his war injuries, he was among the originators of the Israel Disabled War Veterans Organization, fighting for the rights of injured veterans. Later, after eight years as chairman of this organization, he joined the founders of the Israel Sport Center for the Disabled (ISCD) in Ramat Gan, which became a pioneering sports center for disabled individuals. He served as director of the ISCD for thirty-seven years, and then as chairman in a voluntary capacity for many more years.

I followed a similar path, first as secretary of state for Georgia, then as administrator of the United States Veterans Administration, serving wounded veterans, then as senator for Georgia, fighting—among other things—for the social rights of the disabled and, finally, as secretary of the American Battle Monuments Commission.

I find a strong similarity between this book and my own book, *Strong at the Broken Places*, written after my own terrible war injuries.

These two books, in my opinion, complete and complement each other. Moshe's book clearly articulates the sensation of pain and the feeling of approaching death, while my book describes overcoming life-changing shock and loss. Both ultimately celebrate triumph and the power of the human spirit. It is important for every person to know about these things, especially the world's leaders, in whose hands world peace—or war—rests.

The uniqueness of this book is that it gives the reader a precise and realistic view of the horrors of war, and the feelings of the individual who is engulfed by it.

PREFACE

BY ARIK RASHKES

Moshe Rashkes is a war hero, a humanitarian hero, a successful author, and one of the founders of the state of Israel. He is also my father.

My father and his family fled Poland in the late 1920s, due to the increasing number of pogroms and growing anti-Semitism. He was only two years old when his family arrived, with very little money and very few possessions, at the shore of what was then Palestine. They moved to Tel Aviv, where life in the 1930s was far from easy. The family lived in a small one-bedroom apartment, worked double shifts, and went hungry most days—but they felt relatively safe. News from Europe came in sporadically and it carried unimaginable horror, initially from ghettos and later from death camps, and, sadly, included the news that most members of the Rashkes family who had stayed in Poland were either missing—or gone.

As a youngster, my father and his friends understood that in order to survive they would need to fight. It was more than self-defense, it was survival, and fighting for Israel's independence and simple right to exist was not an option, but a duty and a necessity. My father fought on the Jerusalem front and was severely wounded in a heroic battle at the entrance to Sha'ar Hagai, the gate to Jerusalem.

My father's injury transformed his life drastically, and his miraculous rehabilitation formed his philosophy of life and his future. In 1952, he was elected Chairman of the Israel Disabled War Veterans Organization. One of my childhood memories is walking with my father on the main street of Tel Aviv and being stopped time and again by people—strangers to me—who profusely thanked my father for things he did for them. They were veterans and he was fighting for their rights, for their dignity, and for their recognition.

After serving the veterans, he decided to lead and build a sports center for disabled children. He became a major advocate for rehabilitation through sports, applying many of the methodologies that had helped him with his own rehabilitation. Thousands of disabled kids have gone to the Israel Sport Center for the Disabled and it has helped them gain confidence, pride, and success. My father was, and still is, a hero for many of them.

In 1962, my father published his first book. Its Hebrew title translates into English as *Days of Lead*. He once told me that he wrote the book in order to be able to forget. The memories were simultaneously very painful and very important, and the book served as a tool for bringing relief. The book was a major success and an astounding best seller, and praise came pouring in. My father, with barely a high school diploma, had created a masterpiece.

Recently, as my father approached his ninetieth birthday, I asked him if I could translate the book and publish it for the first time in English. This was one of his dreams that had faded into the background over the years because of his busy schedule. This dream is now a reality and it has become one of the best birthday gifts for this wonderful and special occasion. The publishing of the book also coincides with Israel's seventieth anniversary, an event that would never have happened without the spirit and bravery of my father and his fellow soldiers.

CHAPTER 1

THE HILL

Wearily I lifted the field glasses to my eyes. They had once been Ilan's. In front of me stretched emaciated slopes that quivered hazily when I first looked at them, and then settled down and stopped moving. My eyes wandered over the few scraggy clumps of trees scattered over the area, whose shadows made pits of blackness on the rocky ground.

For a moment I blinked my eyes. Between the faded green trees I made out little figures moving back and forth. I took a long, hard look. There was no doubt: enemy soldiers. Groups of them rushing around busily, as if time was short and they were hurrying to carry out their orders. Now I could make out a few lorries standing near them. The soldiers gathered around the lorries and began working frantically. I could even make out the cannons hidden behind the fences. But I was already tired, dead tired.

The words of the company commander hammered against my temples: "Hold the hill—at all costs." That's what he had said before we set out. That's the order we were given. But we didn't have much more left to pay. We were nine when it all started, and now there were only five of us left. Two of them lay dead next to me, their heads smashed into messy pulps of flesh and bones by a machine gun. The commander said something else: "Until reinforcements arrive." But I wasn't sure they'd make it, and was beginning to doubt they were even on their way. When the order had been given, I hadn't realized all its implications. Now I completely understood it. But I was so bone-tired I couldn't even complain. Perhaps reinforcements were really on the way. That's what the company commander told us would happen, after all . . .

The enemy soldiers had stopped rushing about. Soon the shelling would start. I felt it wouldn't be long. A bright tongue of flame glittered through the trees. That was it. I knew the time had come. White smoke hung there like a light cloud, and a shrill whistle cut through the air. A heavy explosion shook its anger loose somewhere on the slope of the hill. Heavy smoke climbed into the sky. It was a marking bomb. The real shelling began after a few trial shots. The explosions began to follow one another. Their thunder rocked and shook the layer of stones on the hill, like an earthquake that wanted to pound every bit of stone into gravel.

At first I could still make out the exploding shells. A dirty gray whirlpool of dust and rocks rose into the air, and fell back to the ground like a hail of debris from a detonation. The more frequent the explosions became, the less I was able to see. The smoke and dust rolling over the rocks mingled into a heavy cloud that hung over the entrenchment and covered the face of the sun. But by this time I wasn't paying any attention to what was happening outside my own limited sphere of interest. I lay on the ground, curled up like a hedgehog, pressing desperately as close to the earth as I could. I would have liked to have been swallowed up in it, to be swallowed by it. I clasped the palms of my hands over the nape of my neck and pressed my arms over my ears in a vain attempt to shut out the thunder of the shells.

The guns continued to slam away at a crazy pace. Cold sweat started trickling over my face. At first it was only my forehead that glistened with sweat, but soon my whole body was washed by the sticky wetness. Streams of it, mixed with dust and smoke, trickled into my eyes, stinging them mercilessly. Every time the thunder of the shots rolled over the shuddering rocks, I shut my eyes. My body shrank into a tight, twisted knot, and my head banged against the ground. When I opened my eyes again, it was like waking up from a nightmare. Everything spun around me, around and around until my head reeled.

This had been going on for hours already. My whole body ached from the sudden contortions. Weakness took hold of me. My stomach lurched and the gorge rose. I felt like vomiting . . . I must have been stunned by the cannon fire and couldn't feel my face. My lips were paralyzed; I bit them but felt nothing, and couldn't feel my throat either. I put out my hand hesitantly and patted my neck. It was smooth and wet. My fingers dabbled in a warm, soft liquid. I passed my hands in front of my eyes, agitated. My fingers were smeared with a mixture of blood and soot. A piece of shrapnel from a shell must have hit me in the neck. But I felt no pain. I just kept on getting weaker and weaker, my strength flowing away.

I heard a muffled sound, a cry, like that of a frightened baby. It was so choked, so far off, so faint. The cries grew louder, came closer, until I could hear them quite clearly. Only a desperately wounded man screams like that, and this hopeless howling roused me from my dazed state. Slowly I turned my head toward the voice. But I could hardly see anything. Everything was covered by thick mist and acrid smoke. I screwed up my eyes and peered into the mist, putting my whole body into the effort of seeing. The dense mist lifted a little, and through its veil, which opened slightly before closing again, curled a heavy cloud of smoke that climbed over the stone outpost on my left. The wounded man's cries grew louder. *Who could it be?* I wondered with growing terror. A chill of fear passed through my body, a chill that deadened the senses.

A black shadow passed in front of the mist. I strained my eyes. Through the rising smoke the figure of a man lurched, running and rocking from side to side, as if he were drunk. At first all I saw was a black shadow. But when the shape came closer I could see someone waving his hands as if he wanted to tell me something, to give me a signal. I couldn't see the ends of his legs. They were covered by the mist that spread over the ground. He seemed to be floating and hovering on the waves of a sooty smoke. His cries didn't grow fainter, but became louder, and his movements became more frantic. Now I could see that he was banging himself on the head, hitting himself and shouting. Another minute and he'd reach me. Only ten strides between us. The sound of the explosions deafened me, but I couldn't take my eyes off him. Suddenly he changed the direction of his walk. He stumbled, swayed in the opposite direction—toward enemy lines.

"Stop!" a hoarse cry burst from my throat. "Stop!" He went on. My voice was lost in the thunder of the guns. I struggled to my feet and ran after him. "Stop!" I went on shouting. "Stop!"

I caught up with him. Now I could put my hand out and catch him. A mighty burst rocked me. I threw myself on him and pulled him down to the ground with me. I bent over his head. His face was wreathed in smoke. It was Gershon! But he looked different. His face was twisted, distorted. His eyes bulged out of their hollows as if they wanted to leap out of the sagging sockets of flesh that held them. His gaze was expressionless, empty, hollow. He didn't seem to see me at all, didn't know me. I felt the shivering of his body against my skin. White foam covered his lips.

"Gershon, what's the matter?" I yelled. His eyes moved over my face indifferently. The whites of his eyes were turned red, shot through by a thick network of veins. His mouth was wide open, and a choked, bitter cry burst from his chest.

"They're dying," he cried. "All of them dying . . ." His eyes were shut tight.

"Who's dying?" I shouted desperately, holding his shoulders with both hands and shaking his body with all my strength. "Answer me! Who's dying?" He didn't reply. But his weeping grew fainter, and his vacant eyes opened again. "What happened?" I asked again. He shook his head weakly.

"I'm going to die," he wailed. "I'm going to die." His face quivered, and his howl turned into a sob.

"Shut up!" I yelled at him, feeling his madness taking hold of me. "Shut up . . . shut up . . ." If only I could have shouted like him, cried, released all the weight of fear that pressed on me. But I couldn't. Something inside me, stronger than I was, prevented me from doing this. Was it sanity that was stopping me? Or madness? I screamed at him in helpless anger: "Shut up! Shut up!"

But he didn't stop crying. His sobs grew louder: "I'm going to die," he wept, "to die . . ."

"You'll die alright, if you don't shut up," I shrieked, at the end of my tether. Seen through my burning eyes, his head became a ball of human flesh that wouldn't stop screaming.

"I'm going to die," the red ball screamed. I put the barrel of my gun to his neck, in a murderous rage, and began pressing. His yells turned into a hoarse, broken rattle, which in turn became a strangled gargle. Spit and foam came from his mouth, and his voice died down.

What was I doing? I stopped pushing the barrel, in alarm. Gershon drew a little air into his lungs. A rasping groan and suppressed fit of coughing shook his chest. His eyes remained fixed on me. Then he turned over so that he was lying on his stomach, sobbing quietly to himself.

The shelling stopped. The thunder of the explosions grew fainter, but went on echoing across the hills. That was a bad omen. Soon the enemy infantry would start to attack. This interval was curiously relaxing: a sort of calm accompanied by a feeling that retribution was on the way. It hung in the air, like a cloud over my head. Soon it would burst on top of me.

The machine guns from the nearby hill began barking in measured anger, like a pack of mad dogs. A hail of whistling bullets slammed into the rocks. Their furious, monotonous whine cracked against my ears. I wriggled my body into as small a shape as possible and lay on the earth, clutching pieces of it in my hands. A terrible, dull, abysmal fear of losing my grip on the soil seized me. Because my face was squashed against the ground, I stared right at the slivers of stone scattered in front of me. They seemed to be getting bigger, longer, until they were as high as lofty mountains whose peaks were out of sight. I was tiny compared to them. I couldn't climb them. My hands and feet turned to stone. Heavy lead had engulfed them.

The machine guns were silent now. My senses started coming back, and my staccato breathing grew a little steadier. Weak, crowded voices flowed in from afar, as if they came from the bowels of the earth. They grew louder and became an angry uproar: the enemy's battle sounds. Whistles blew, and voices shouted guttural cries of encouragement. The voices came closer. They were climbing the slope. Through the mist it was hard to see what was happening. All I could make out was the blurred shape of the sun, enveloped in clouds of smoke. The commotion grew louder, and the sound of a new kind of shot joined in: the chatter of machine guns firing single volleys. The sense of approaching danger wouldn't let me stay there. I had to see what was happening. I glanced at Gershon. He was breathing heavily. I shook him firmly.

"Try to get to the first-aid station," I shouted in his ear. His face still showed no expression. I pushed him with my foot to get him moving, and then I started crawling forward. I turned my head toward him for a last look. He began crawling on all fours, like a robot set in motion, toward the rock outside the smoke.

I straightened up and peered over the rock carefully. I could see down the slope. Figures . . . shapes . . . movement . . . Two lines of soldiers pushed upward relentlessly, checkered keffiyehs flapping around their heads in the wind. My heart beat faster as I watched the crouching figures and the way their bent knees rose and fell. The hundred meters that separated us didn't prevent me from sensing the heavy rhythm of their breathing. They panted through their gaping mouths and screamed with all the strength of their lungs as they fired off shots from the machine guns and rifles held next to their hips. A cloud of dust, the dust from the rocks chipped by the hail of bullets, moved in front of them.

They were coming closer, a broad chain of soldiers surrounding the hill on three sides. I could see the expressions on their faces quite clearly; fatigue, anger, and hatred etched in them. Or was it only a mirage? For a moment I was tempted to think so. I closed my eyes . . . a babel of cries, the roar of shots . . . my eyes opened again. I couldn't take my eyes off the black muzzles of the guns held in their hands. They frightened me. So black and deep . . . One of the dark circles came up to me rapidly, growing and expanding until it looked like the angry mouth of a volcano, which omitted fire and smoke. The thunder of the machine guns made my whole body shudder and transfixed me to the spot. My heart beat crazily until I felt my arteries were going to burst. What was the matter with me? Fear? I didn't know. Nausea seized me. My stomach turned over, my head was thudding, my temples were about to burst.

I gripped my machine gun weakly. I had to do something . . . I had to act . . . to do something . . . to move . . . To rid myself of the paralysis that was seeping through me . . . To shoot! I had to shoot at the enemy, although I didn't have much of a chance of getting away with it. But I had to try!

But why weren't our guns firing? I glanced to my right, at the low stone outpost next to the poplar tree. The stones at the lip were chipped. Nothing left of the place. I could only see part of a machine gun. It lay upside down between the slivers of stone that nearly covered it. What about the men in the outpost? I screwed up my eyes and straightened up to get a better look. Bullets whistled above me, but I hardly heard them. What about the men in the post—Yosef, Hayim, and Sasson? Were they alright? The case of ammunition lay on its side. Sasson's powerful body leaned against it, motionless. I couldn't see his face. His head lay inside the box. He was dead alright. Like the rest of them. Next to him lay Hayim, flat on his back, his hands held out to the sides as if he was trying to say, "What more could I do?"

Movement. Something was moving on the heap of stones. A figure emerged from behind the fallen heap. Yosef moved about, his one hand groping in the air, trying to find a way out. His other hand was clasped over his eyes. "Orderly! Orderly!" he cried out as he crept up the slope of the hill. He might be able to reach the first-aid station near the road. Might make it . . .

They were coming closer. Their shoes clattered over the stones. This is how the hangman's steps sound to the condemned. A giant foot in a hobnailed boot with long, shining iron spikes moved toward me. The boot was coming down, coming down on my writhing body, crushing me. The iron spikes sank deep into my flesh. A cold chill passed through me, the chill of living flesh crushed by cold, sharp steel. What a horrible feeling.

I leaped wildly in the direction of the post, with its abandoned machine gun. The ground around me shook with bullets, which buzzed like a swarm of troublesome wasps. I went on running. That was the only chance of escaping from the ring of soldiers closing in on me: to move on. I couldn't stop. I rushed toward the post and banged into it, falling so hard that I pushed aside Hayim's still body. I pulled the machine gun madly out of the pile of shattered stones that almost covered it. I pulled it out and cradled it in my arms. The chill of the wooden barrel, which I put next to my cheek, encouraged me: its pleasant touch gave me strength and hope. I hugged the machine gun, feeling my pulse beat against its iron body. I held it longingly, clinging tightly and trying to merge with it, to make it part of me.

The machine gun's barrel rose. My hands had lifted it. It was almost as if they had gained independent life and will and were acting separately from the other parts of my body, which were drawn to the ground and clung to it. My right hand held the handle of the gun, and my finger squeezed the steel trigger. It made me feel better. The machine gun barked. Its butt made my shoulder shudder. Tongues of flame and smoke flickered from the jerking mouth. On the other side of the gun sights, I could see the astonished faces of the enemy soldiers spread out in front of me. They dropped to the ground quickly and took shelter. The machine gun rattled on. I fired at every hillock and bush, my senses reeling. Fired for all I was worth. The field was empty. Nobody there. They'd all gone into hiding. Only the officers' voices went on echoing.

The machine gun stopped firing: the magazine was used up. I reached my hand to the case of ammunition lying on its side. My palm snaked into it and froze on the spot. The case was empty. No ammunition. That was the end. The stones in front of me suddenly became as tall as the soldiers who pushed forward with cries of triumph, which turned into a deep wail. My eyes were fixed on the enemy soldiers. Their strained faces hunted my gaze. Swarthy and bathed in gleaming sweat. Their mouths opened in a yell, which bared their white teeth.

The awareness of my coming end made every movement of theirs seem slower, as if they were crawling. It might only have been the effect of the burning sun shining in my eyes. The heat . . . the heat . . . The burning machine gun, which I still held, was radiating some of its heat. The stones I lay on burned like coals. Fatigue seized me, dulling my senses like a drug, dulling the pain and sorrow of leaving life. In reconciling myself to this, I felt no regret or despair, just acceptance of my fate. At this moment a sudden inner urge dominated me. Hurriedly I collected the hand grenades from the belts of the dead men next to me. I pulled out their pins frantically and threw the grenades at the enemy.

The grenades I threw exploded. The attacking enemy soldiers were swallowed up behind the stones once more. But they kept up their guttural cries: whispering voices, the groans of wounded men, and loud shouts of command. They were fixed to the ground, not moving. I felt a sudden twinge of contempt for them. What were they waiting for? Why were they delaying the end? But as long as I had a breath of life left in my body, there was only one thing I wanted. I had always cowered at the touch of iron. Even as a boy I hated the touch of metal against my skin. It made me shudder. When two pieces of iron were scraped against one another, it annoyed me and gave me gooseflesh. That's all I asked for: could I die now, without feeling the iron touch me, without the hated metal tearing my flesh?

Of the four grenades I had collected, there was only one left. I looked at it affectionately. My whole world was concentrated in this small round lump of iron. My fingers closed on it, held it tightly. I brought it up close to my eyes, next to my burning face. The iron squares on the outer casing looked like a crossword puzzle. A puzzle whose answer was life or death. At that moment an idea flashed into my head: killing myself. The grenade, my last friend in the outpost, would help me carry out this last wish. Suddenly its touch became soft and relaxing. No, it wasn't made of metal. It was gentle and soft. This idea appealed to me so much that I felt I was going to break into a shout of joy, like a mischievous child. They wouldn't have the pleasure of killing me. No, I'd spoil that for them. I began pulling the pin out, and relaxed my tense grip.

Suddenly, a shock aroused my whole body, a hidden memory came to light in me, flowed inside me, made me tense and alert. My hand clenched the grenade once more, and my fingers stroked its bulging shape. A spark of life. Why should I die? There was a bag full of hand grenades in the little stone post on top of the hill, about twenty paces away. I sprinted there, jumping over the rocks and thorn bushes. The bullets whizzed around me. The stubborn chatter of the machine guns had a dry, cruel twang. I rushed forward, throwing myself with all my strength onto the stones in front of me.

I slid forward on the jagged stones, until stopped by a large rock that blocked my path. I went on crawling. My hand was cut and my face scratched and bruised. The rough ground cut my nose and lips. My hands and knees were sticky with blood. My palm was still clenched around the grenade, but I went on dragging myself toward my goal. Every movement of my body seemed to last for hours. How much longer would I have to drag myself? The ten strides that still lay ahead seemed like a long trek, endless . . .

My ears were blocked, and I couldn't hear the sounds of the explosions. All I could hear was my labored breathing. In front of me was a winding passage surrounded by stones piled high. I crawled inside it. It was so narrow that I felt my breath coming back at me from the walls. A rush of hot, damp air struck me in the face, like a summer wind. I lifted my head quickly. Two frightened black eyes were fixed on me. An enemy soldier!

The contact of our eyes was enough for me to take in every tremor of his face. The wide-open eyes that stared at me were afraid and taken by surprise. It's strange how quickly one's thoughts work. He aroused a feeling of pity in me. Was it because I had already reconciled myself to my fate, that I could allow myself so much compassion toward him? Had despair driven the fear out of me? He was young, about my age. Perhaps a few years older. I was sorry for him. Was he a fellah, a villager? It looked like it. His skin was swarthy, his white teeth gleamed healthily. No, they were not as healthy as I had at first thought. Spots of black rot showed in his two front teeth. I could also make out a crown of shining gold in the back of his mouth. Perhaps he wasn't a fellah after all?

Our glances broke away from one another. I had to carry on! Each of us would fight for his life. That is the rule of war. I felt no hatred for him and would have preferred him to just disappear, to run away. But he was in my way, and I had to destroy him. Suddenly he vanished from my sight—but not from my senses. I knew exactly where he was. He had retreated to the other side of the rock. I had no doubt that he was aiming his gun at the passage at this very moment. He was waiting for me to walk into his trap.

I clambered lightly over the rock, and from there, I sprang to the other side with a sudden leap. I threw myself with all my might onto the place where he was probably hiding. While I was still falling through the air, I saw him pressed against the side of the rock. He was squatting on his knees and elbows, his gun aimed at the passage as I had guessed. I fell onto his back. One of my hands was stretched out to push away the submachine gun that he turned toward me. The other hand, which still held the grenade, came down on the back of his neck with terrific force. The grenade acted like a club. A heavy, dull crunch, like a nut being cracked open, mingled with a choked groan of pain: "Aaahhh." The gun fell out of the soldier's hands, and he fell, face downward. A violent twitch pulled his head down between his shoulders. I went on beating his head with the grenade, as hard as I could. After every blow, he gave a choked rattle. Jets of warm blood spurted over my face and hands. I continued smashing the grenade down on his skull with uncontrollable anger. I was half-mad by that time. My clothes were red with his blood. They soaked through with it. He tried to move, with the last drop of his strength, to stretch his hand out toward the gun that lay in front of him. But a crushing blow to his skull put an end to that.

The grenade in my hand was red. Blood dripped from it. The warm touch of the blood made me even more insane. Without knowing why, I pulled the pin of the grenade. A click. The wick lit up with a hiss. Four seconds left until the explosion, but it seemed as if hours went by without the grenade going off. I lost all sense of time. His blood-spattered head hung in front of my eyes. He was my enemy and had wanted to kill me. Here was his gun, which he had aimed at me. But I had gotten him first. His friends weren't very far away. They were out for my blood. I heard the rustle of their approaching steps, steps coming closer.

The grenade . . . I threw it at the soldiers creeping toward me, threw as hard as I could. It exploded in the air with a sharp, strident blast, like a giant whip cracked over the hills, followed by an angry clap of thunder that echoed around the valley. Cries of pain from behind the rocks. The splinters of the grenade must have hit them. I had to get to the bag of grenades. On a sudden impulse, I picked up the machine gun that was lying on the ground, and rose to my feet, firing in all directions, firing and yelling with all the strength of my lungs. I ran along like this, shooting and shouting furiously, until I ran into the stone fence. I stumbled over it and rolled over into the outpost beyond it. The gun fell out of my hands and struck me on the head.

Dizziness. Black and red circles whirled and galloped before my eyes. Their orbits grew smaller, until they stopped spinning altogether, and the great metallic dome of the sky showed again above my stinging eyes. It wasn't over yet. I looked around me. The post. The bag of grenades lay on its side, propped against the fallen wall of stone. I stretched out my hand to the bag, and the grenades spilled out, striking the ground with a heavy, muf-fled sound.

Automatically, I took hold of the first grenade my hand touched. I pulled the pin out and threw it over the wall. I went on throwing the grenades, picking them up from the ground and tossing them feverishly, one after the other. Through the boom of the detonations, I heard broken cries. I didn't know what they were. Were they human voices? A sudden movement near a thorn bush a few yards away brought me to my knees. I kept my eyes on the bush. It moved, and I threw a grenade at it. As the grenade spun toward it and my arm came down again, two soldiers peered out from between the thorns. I could see them crouching there, like taut springs. But I could also see the black muzzles of the guns in their hands, pointed straight at me. I threw myself backward and pulled my head down.

A white, clear light flashed in the muzzle, a quick, light flash, like the flame of a candle flickering in the wind. Then sharp and terrible lightning struck me, struck me like a raging storm, and a crushing, howling wind burst over me. A mighty blow shook my whole body. I was thrown backward, blinded. Darkness, a deep blackness in whose vast space flickers of flame spat, showering sparks over me. They fell on me, exploding on my head.

I couldn't breathe. My lungs were clenched in a painful vise. I struggled to take in a little air, but couldn't shake free. A gust of heat began spreading through my chest and blowing through my body, my arteries, spreading like a licking flame. I felt hot spouts of blood filling the hollows of my chest and belly, rising up to my gasping throat, my blocked nose. I kept trying to breathe, to suck in some air, to wriggle out of the ring of suffocation pressing on my throat and lungs. But I couldn't get any. Blood and spit spurted from my mouth.

My head hung to one side, humming and buzzing spasmodically. A grating noise pounded in my ears like a rusty saw, and drops fell softly somewhere in my bursting skull. Drums roared against my temples—loud drums. They swelled up into a crescendo. I pressed my burning cheeks against the sunbaked stones. I felt their cool, smooth surface. My lips quivered in longing for a little moisture. I held them against the stones, which still held some of the spit and blood I had vomited up. I sucked the wet stones thirstily. They gave me a few minutes of chill relief. But soon their cool touch became a feeling of burning fire. The fire of thirst.

Thirst . . . I was boiling all over. A bellows blew in my veins, blowing heat and flame. My tongue burned, my parched palate was on fire. My throat was choked by the mixture of spit and salty blood. The darkness that covered my eyes gradually lifted. Its place was taken by the dim image of the sun. I could feel its warmth through my closed eyes. It came closer and closer to me, a ball of fire—turning and boiling, swirling and blazing—until it became a huge purple spider, which put its white-hot hands on me, clasped my shrinking body, and vomited a sea of molten lava into me. I was burning, scorching! All the moisture in my body had gone. In another minute my flesh would burst, like land tormented by drought. "Water! Water!" But my voice choked and faded away. My dry lips moved up and down, but I couldn't make a sound.

Agonizing pains squeezed my chest. A bayonet of white-hot steel pierced my lungs, twisting cruelly in the wound. And then dozens of sharp knives stuck into me, cutting my living, quivering flesh—cutting, twisting, and tearing. With the last of my strength, I tried to escape the sharp points. But I couldn't. They cut me angrily, devoured my flesh. Devoured me limb by limb . . .

Tired. No strength left. My chest and lungs swelled up with the blood that flooded them. My hands were weak and soft. My heart beat slowly. The arteries were empty: the streams of burning blood had flowed out. A drowsy fatigue enveloped me, and I felt myself falling asleep, sinking into a redeeming slumber. I knew that I was going to die. Soon I wouldn't feel anything. I sank quietly into a dark, cool cave. Fell down and down. My head felt dizzy. Everything was dark and black. Only one small spot of light glistened above my head. There was the mouth of the cave. But I was going far away . . . far away . . .

I was only eighteen, and already departing from life. Going . . . I saw the misty shapes of my mother and father. They approached me with hesitant steps. Their trembling hands were held out toward me. Their faces were lined with sorrow, and their backs bent with mourning. They pleaded: "Come back, son, come back!" They begged me. They were crying.

I continued falling and receding from them. I waved to them wearily, trying to say something to wipe away their tears. But I couldn't. My voice had gone. I loved them, and wanted to comfort them. I was sorry for them. I was tired. I drew away from them and sank still further. Sank down . . . sank . . .

The single spot of light over my head had also gone. Complete darkness surrounded me. I could hear a weak, soft wail somewhere. A long wail, the sound of a trumpet. A wailing trumpet.

Everything was blurred. All falling to pieces. The darkness lost its black color and became hollow. It wiped everything out, this darkness. But the shadows were stronger than it. Figures came out of the dark mist, blurred figures. Quivering clouds reminded me of something. But what? Who?

Who was I?

The events of my life flashed in front of me with giddy speed: faces, like the reflection of a small, laughing boy. His black hair waved in the strong, wailing wind. The trumpet moaned. His blue eyes laughed.

The images changed. Came and hurried on. A boy in his teens. A smile of compassion playing at the corners of his mouth. Everything was going around and around. Faces of people in the whirlpool . . . people . . . human beings . . . my own face.

What was I doing here? . . . The war . . . the war . . .

The visions chased one another. Everything was happening so quickly. The war . . .

CHAPTER 2

THE CAMP

"This war isn't going to last long," Yehuda said. "It'll soon be over. You can take my word for it." His eyes glittered with enthusiasm, and there was a hint of derision in their corners. Was it aimed at me? Because I was stuck there in the training camp, far from the places where the real fighting was going on?

"You really think so?" I asked hesitantly.

"What a question!" Yehuda gave me a knowing wink. "We'll finish them off right away!"

His confident voice made me feel ashamed. I wanted to open my mouth, to protest. But he stopped me with a decisive gesture. "In general I'm fed up with training greenhorns. This training camp isn't my line." I nodded in agreement. "I'm going to the front," he added. "Must get a few shots in before the whole thing's over."

"Yes, you're right," I muttered. "I'm also fed up."

"I'm leaving camp tomorrow," he snorted proudly.

"Has the camp commander agreed?" I asked, taken aback.

"Listen to me," he retorted with a swagger. "That Old Ramrod cuts no ice with me. I just forgot how to train the men. I lost my memory, get it? So, he had to get rid of me." My astonished look only increased his flow of words. "Look, chum," he went on, "I wasn't born yesterday!" His eyes rested on me for a moment while he savored his triumph. It was almost as if he was asking me, "Aren't I terrific?"

"You certainly know the ropes," I said with envy. "I just haven't got the courage to get away with tricks like that. The only thing I can do is to ask Ramrod for a transfer to a combat unit . . . Think I've got a chance?"

"Huh!" Yehuda snorted. "You're just wasting your time. You've got to be smart, on the ball—like me. Else you'll stay right here. The OC will keep you in camp until the war's over."

"Rubbish," the platoon commander, Arthur, chimed in. "You boys are just looking for trouble." And he added, in a strict tone, "What do you need it for? Do what you're told to do, and don't poke your nose where it's not wanted."

"He's dead right," added Yehiel, the instructor, who was standing next to us. "War isn't a game of tag. Don't be so anxious to get to the front." He put his hand in his pocket and pulled out a photograph.

"Have you seen this?" he asked.

"No, I haven't."

Yehiel held it out to me. "These are our boys. The enemy's spreading it around."

I glanced at it, and my blood froze. I felt like choking. Paralyzed. Our soldiers: a heap of naked bodies, their limbs cut off; a smashed white hand, fingers clenched, stuck into the air as if trying to grasp it; drops of clotting blood trickling over their pale skin. Our boys . . . The photograph shook in my hands. Heads bashed in, with ears cut off. Black splotches covered their faces. I looked desperately for their eyes, or at least for the place where the eyes should be, but they weren't there. Instead I saw hollow black pits, dark caves. Their feet had also been cut off. Ropes were tied around their waists. "No, no," The sight left my hands and feet trembling and gave me a feeling of weakness and slackness in my muscles.

"I've seen atrocity pictures before," Arthur said. "Those shots of the German concentration camps. Naked bodies, gas chambers, rows of corpses lying in trenches. You must have seen them."

"Yes."

"Well, that's what war's like. Perhaps it's the symbol of fate. If you'd been in the camps, you might have been dead too. But you're here, in Tel Aviv."

"It's all a question of luck," Yehiel summed up. He took the photograph from me and stuffed it back in his pocket.

"It couldn't happen to me," I blurted out.

"Why not?" Arthur jeered. He took a pipe out of his shirt pocket, knocked it against his palm, and emptied out the stale tobacco. I was silent. A fatherly smile spread over his face, as if he wanted to say: "Really, my boy, you don't know what you're talking about."

I coughed slightly, to indicate that I didn't agree with him. "Well, I'll be seeing you," I said abruptly, strolling to the center of the camp.

Near the parade ground stood Old Ramrod, looking at the recruits passing by. He was staring at a group of greenhorns, standing next to the taps outside the dining room, who had just finished cleaning their messtins. "Hey, you there!" the OC shouted. "Don't you intend to turn off these taps?" The greenhorns, who wore faded, threadbare clothes, stopped in their tracks, panic-stricken, and gazed at him like a flock of frightened ducks. "Is that how you behave at home, too?" he yelled. The recruits stood rooted to one spot, unable to move. "Well, hurry up and turn off those taps at once!" he roared impatiently. They hurried to the dripping taps, their boots spattering mud over their trousers as they closed them. Then they made for their huts, leaving trails of mud behind.

I came up to Ramrod. Suddenly he turned to me, in a movement that took me by surprise.

"Well?" he asked. "Want something?"

"I w-w-wanted to talk to you," I stammered.

"Then come to my office at one," he dismissed me.

————

At one o'clock I presented myself in his office. Ramrod was standing behind a broad desk. He gestured to a chair, and I sat down slowly.

"Well, what's it all about?" he asked, fixing a stern eye on me.

His penetrating stare scattered all my thoughts, and I didn't know how to begin.

"Well?" he encouraged me.

"You see, here in the camp . . ." The words stuck in my throat. I breathed deeply and raised my voice: "I want to go off to the front . . . to fight . . . like all the others . . . To leave the camp . . ."

His lips clenched in a worried expression. "Listen," he growled in quite a kindly tone, "the war's only just begun. There's no need to hurry." He stopped abruptly, leaned back in his chair, and went on in a soft voice: "And don't think that our soldiers will always be in rags, as they are now, without proper uniforms, without enough arms. The day will come when all these things will change."

"But . . . but . . ." I mumbled, confused and unsure of myself.

The OC cut me short: "I don't intend to keep you against

your will." He went on in an angry voice: "Think about it until tomorrow, and then, if you still want to leave, you can go." His voice hinted that our talk was over.

"Right," I said. I got up from my chair like someone who had just had a tongue-lashing, and went outside.

Arthur was standing on the porch. "Well, did you see him?" he questioned me.

"Yes, I've just been there."

"So?"

"I want to leave."

A shadow of disappointment crossed his face. "You need this like a hole in your head," he said, and stalked off.

I was more determined than ever to go—now that Old Ramrod and Arthur had both tried to persuade me to stay. As if I suspected they were trying to deprive me of a valuable and rare experience. It was true that the photograph Yehiel had shown me had put me off for a while. But its shocking effect was wearing off: the picture had become a collection of faded images, details that had no connection with one another, like a tune that one remembers vaguely but can't hum from beginning to end although it rings in one's ears.

Did I really want to go to the front? Was that really what I wanted? For a moment I almost changed my mind. After all, Old Ramrod was also against it. Could I go back to him and tell him I had decided to stay? I walked off to the fence at the end of the camp, thinking about this.

A group of soldiers walked past me quickly. Their clothes flapped as they marched, a collection of old clothes bought from a secondhand dealer. All different shades of khaki. And the hats . . . Each of them wore a different kind of knitted woolen cap. I looked at myself. Tight khaki trousers and a thin olive-green shirt.

I had brought these clothes from home. That was two months ago, and I hadn't been given a uniform yet. *How much longer will this go on?*

My thoughts were confused, and this made everything seem gloomy and miserable. The skies were overcast. The cool wind made my teeth chatter. The middle of winter—and I didn't have a coat. Until then I hadn't bothered much about things like that, despite the rain that had already fallen twice during outdoor training sessions. The recruits complained every time they were soaked by these sudden bursts of rain. I would open my shirt to the falling drops, as if I wanted to get soaked through to my bones, and call out: "That's the way to get tough, boys!" As it grew colder, we ran in the rain, clothes stuck tight to our bodies, our teeth chattering. Although we wallowed in mud for hours on end, not a single man fell ill.

But now I felt the cold more than ever before. I could have asked for a short leave so that I could go to my parents' home and fetch a coat. But wearing a civilian coat would have spoiled my military appearance—or so I thought. And then I imagined my parents' puzzled looks if I arrived home in the dead of winter wearing light summer things.

"Why aren't you wearing a coat?" they had asked me anxiously the last time I had been home.

To which I replied casually: "I have to get tough, to get used to little things like that." And when I noticed their skeptical look, I went off to the bathroom to have a cold shower. "You see," I called to them boastfully, coming out shivering with cold, "I'm getting used to it!"

But my father continued looking at me suspiciously. "Do you have enough clothes and food?" he asked.

"Of course, Dad," I declared confidently. "What do you think?"

His skeptical expression told me I had not succeeded in dispelling his suspicions. This prompted me to add: "You can see I'm getting used to suffering. Spartan education."

"Why not take the coat, all the same?" my mother said in a tender voice, holding it out to me. I refused it with pretended annoyance, although inwardly I would have liked to have taken it.

"No, I don't need it!" I protested. "Please let me alone. I don't need anything." They looked at me sorrowfully as I left.

But now I really missed the coat. My skin was rough, like a chicken whose feathers have been plucked. Perhaps I was scared? Afraid to leave the camp? Was I going to change my mind? . . . I turned back, as if running away from my doubts, and returned to the OC's office.

"I want to see the OC," I snapped at the secretary.

"But you've just seen him."

"Yes, I know. But . . . it's something important."

She smiled and walked into his office. In a moment she was back. "OK . . . go right in."

Old Ramrod didn't seem surprised to see me again so soon.

"I came to tell you," I blurted out quickly, "that I've decided to go."

"You've decided?"

"Yes, yes," I mumbled nervously.

"Good, if that's the way you want it." A sad smile appeared on his face. He was silent for a moment, as if he was thinking about something far away. "This afternoon you'll be transferred to the Sarona camp. There you will present yourself to the camp commander. They need platoon commanders." The OC seemed to be choosing his words carefully. "I'm sure you'll make a good fighter," he ended. Silence. We looked at one another. The old battle-scarred soldier, and the untried young star who

was anxious to get a taste of war. Our eyes met. This meeting
of our eyes meant a lot to me: it was a sort of pact between two
generations of warriors, a silent agreement to what I considered
to be the duties and privileges imposed upon every generation in
turn. I regarded myself as representing enthusiasm and strength,
while Ramrod stood for experience and advice. I knew that the
war in which I was going to take part would be a life-or-death
struggle. But I didn't care. At that moment I regarded the need
to face the danger of death as one of my deepest desires. Without
this experience, I wouldn't be a man, and I wouldn't be worthy
of continuing the soldierly tradition that I had just joined, in the
silent pact with the OC.

"I hope we'll meet again," Ramrod said as we parted and
shook hands warmly.

"I hope so too," I echoed as I marched out. His eyes followed
me. "Hope to see you," I mumbled again, dodging outside. The
secretary, who was standing outside the door, glanced at me
curiously.

"Well, what happened?" she asked.

"I'm going to the front," I announced proudly.

"What do you say!" she called out in surprise. "The old man
must be in a good mood today!"

I went to my room, collected my few belongings, and stuffed
them into my kit bag. I loaded it onto my back and went outside
to inform the platoon commander of my transfer. I found him
near the camp, watching a group of soldiers being taught how to
throw hand grenades.

"What're you doing here with a kit bag?" he asked.

"Well, I got what I wanted," I replied.

"What's that?" Arthur exclaimed, as if he couldn't believe
his ears.

"Yes, Ramrod's transferred me to a combat unit. I'm on my way now."

"And what do you say about that?" he barked.

"I'm saying nothing," I answered with ill-concealed pride. "I'm leaving right away, and no regrets. This is my big chance."

"Yes, yes," Arthur grumbled to himself. From sheer force of habit, he pulled out his pipe. "I wish you the best of luck," he added, before putting the pipe into his mouth. He came up to me and patted me on the shoulder. "So you made it, huh?" We shook hands, and then I lifted my kit bag and went off. Arthur followed me with his eyes, clenching his pipe tightly.

About half an hour later, I reached the company's headquarters at Sarona. A group of soldiers was working with two machine guns placed on the ground. "Where's the OC's office?" I asked the instructor. He didn't reply, but pointed to a nearby two-story building with a red-tiled roof. I went into the corridor of the first floor. A cardboard sign hung on one of the doors. I looked at it: "Company Adjutant's Office" it proclaimed in red chalk letters. I knocked at the door.

"Come in!" a choir of voices called out. I went inside, and found several instructors clustered around the adjutant's table. He was giving rapid-fire answers to questions that came at him from all sides. He didn't notice me. I came up to the table and shouted in a loud voice: "Hullo!" He looked up at me in surprise.

"Well?" he muttered, as if annoyed at being disturbed.

"I'm here!" I proclaimed triumphantly, expecting him to share my joy. But he looked at me as if he didn't understand what was going on. "I'm reporting for duty," I added, lowering my voice, embarrassed.

"Oh . . . you're reporting for duty," he mumbled, looking through the papers scattered on the table. Suddenly he raised his head as if he had remembered something. "Yes, of course, you're being transferred to Jerusalem. You'll talk to the company commander in a moment." He dashed into the commander's office with rapid steps, as if he was doing a dance. When he came out a minute later, he announced: "You can go in now."

I entered the room, my heart beating with excitement. The commander welcomed me with a charming smile. He inspected me with his peaceful blue eyes like a good-hearted school teacher looking at his favorite pupil. "Sit down, please," he said calmly. He picked up a packet of cigarettes from the desk and held it out to me.

"No thanks," I said. "I don't smoke."

The OC took a cigarette, lit it slowly, and drew smoke into his lungs. He breathed the smoke in with enjoyment, as if freeing himself of a heavy pressure that squeezed his lungs. "I'm sending you to Jerusalem." He stopped, to test my reaction, and then went on: "It won't be a picnic up there." A slight smile spread across the corners of his mouth. "But I'm sure you'll do a good job there with your platoon."

A wave of joy swept over me. I felt like a schoolboy whose teacher had just taken him out in front of the class and said: "Excellent! Full marks!"

"Your first headache will be how to get to Jerusalem," he went on. "The road is blocked, but occasionally convoys get through. Try to get onto one of those tomorrow. When you get there, contact Erez, the commander of the platoon, in the Building of the Pillars. That's on the main street, you know. Take some leave right away so that you can say goodbye to your folks, and don't forget to take warm clothes with you. It's cold up in the mountains, very cold." I nodded. "OK then. Tomorrow morning at six." He rose and shook hands with me warmly. "Goodbye."

When I went out, the adjutant gave me a travel pass.

"So long," I said to him happily as I left.

"We might still meet again" he said, with a rather mysterious tone in his voice. That evening I said goodbye to my parents. "I'm being transferred to Jerusalem," I remarked casually, adding immediately afterward, in a reassuring voice: "Nothing to worry about."

They looked at me sadly. "Do you have to go?"

"Yes, of course," I made light of the whole matter. "But it's really nothing dangerous."

"Look after yourself, my boy," my father said, patting my back encouragingly. "War isn't a game, you know."

"And don't forget to pray every day," my mother added in a pleading voice.

"You know I don't pray as often as you do." I wanted to show her that my new job wasn't risky.

But she gave me a sad look, and when she saw I was still stubborn, she said: "Alright, then I'll pray for you. I'll pray every day." She added, "Take warm clothes . . . I'll get a few things ready for you," doing her best to stop herself from bursting into tears.

"It's not necessary. Really not," I tried to calm her. "I'm not going to the end of the world. Don't worry. Please."

"At least take the coat," my mother said in a voice choked by tears, holding it out to me. I couldn't refuse. I took it protestingly and kissed her on her forehead. They both hugged me warmly.

As I left the house, they waved to me until I turned the corner.

CHAPTER 3

THE CONVOY

The next day I set off for Jerusalem with the convoy taking supplies to the besieged city. Trucks waited in line on the road. Great clumsy iron cranes protruded from them like masts. Soldiers wearing knitted woolen caps leaned against the armored car at the head of the queue. They gave me a casual glance and went back to their talk.

"Our armored cars aren't worth a damn," one of them complained. "The bullets cut through them like butter." To me the gray armor plating of the waiting cars looked strong and powerful. But the soldier obviously didn't think so.

"You're wrong," another soldier said. "Only really big shells can get through them."

They gave me a questioning look. "Are you coming with us?" one of them asked. I nodded.

"You know," another man said, with a wink at the others, "by the time we get to Jerusalem we'll all be spitting blood." They all laughed heartily. I forced a smile.

"Right, let's move," someone said. We all climbed aboard the truck.

The convoy set off. I felt uncomfortable. Above my head

there was an opening. I stretched my hand out to it and let some cool air in. The winter wind eased the close feeling that made it so hard to breathe. I smiled at the five other fellows in the truck. They noted the expression on my face with sardonic interest.

"New?" asked the baggy-clothed soldier who sat next to me.

"More or less," I answered.

"When you come to Sha'ar Hagai you'll have a chance to learn something."

"Yes, we'll get a hot reception," his mate added. Again, I forced a smile to my lips, taking a long, deep breath. The expression of peace and unconcern on their faces made me wonder if they weren't trying to pull my leg.

I felt as if I was being held in a deep, dark, narrow cellar. The steel walls pressed against me. It was stifling. I could almost feel the air with my hand. Was that how the others had also felt when they traveled in an armored car for the first time?

I looked at my watch. Eight o'clock. I peered out through the open roof covering. The convoy was roaring after us: iron shapes groaning along and letting off streams of smoke behind. I turned my face the other way. A row of high mountains stretching as far as the eye could see, forming a gray, heavy mass. A continent of mountains towering up to the skies. Enemy territory. Breezy morning mists blew lightly over the peaks of the mountains, as if they wanted to hide what was happening there.

The cool wind burned my lips. I wrapped myself in my coat, but the cold still came through. For a moment it occurred to me that my mother was right when she insisted I take the coat. I wondered whether the sudden cold spell meant we were in for some rain. I glanced upward. Rough-edged clouds floated across the heavens. As they moved, their shapes changed. For a moment I tried to find some resemblance between the shapes of the clouds and the shapes of animals and objects: the face of a lion, a frog, a dragon. The brush of a malicious artist splashed its drops across the canvas of the skies.

"We're not far from Ekron," the radio operator remarked in his confident voice. Now the convoy left the tarred road and took the dirt track leading to the village of Ekron. We slowed down. The rains that had fallen there had turned the sandy soil into a viscous quagmire of squishy mud. The trucks slid to the side of the road. The armored cars rushed up to pull them from the mud, with the help of wire cables. We crawled along at a snail's pace.

After two exasperating hours of hard work, the leading armored car announced a half-hour break. The trucks and cars gathered in the main street of the village. Through the open windows of the small white houses peeped the heads of boys and girls, while the men gathered outside in the street, next to the trucks.

The drivers made a hurried inspection of their motors and then went into the café at the corner. The boys who shared my armored car also went along. "Aren't you coming with us?" they asked me as they went out.

"No thanks, I'll stay here."

I went out through the open door and remained standing in the street. My eyes strayed to the hills of Jerusalem. I had a strange feeling, as if somewhere far off in the peaks of those mountains the enemy was watching us.

The weather improved, and the sun emerged from the tattered clouds. I went on looking at the high mountain ridge; here rocks and green forests joined together in an impressive panorama. A spark of light flashed there and went off immediately. It flickered again, and then again. Heliograph signals. My feeling hadn't been wrong. The enemy was watching us. I walked over to the leading armored car and reported what I had seen.

"Yes," the report operator said, "we noticed the signals and asked for an aerial patrol. A Piper plane will pass over Sha'ar Hagai in about fifteen minutes."

I went back to my place. The flicker of the heliograph stopped. Meanwhile everybody was getting ready for the next stage of the journey. The drivers and armored car men went back to their vehicles.

"What are you standing there for, like a bloody pole?" one of them jeered at me. I told him. "Oh, we know the Piper's reconnaissance flights," he sneered. "Those little one-horse planes. Every time, they go over and tell us the land's clear and they can't see a thing. Then later on we find out there's an Arab behind every rock."

Another soldier chimed in: "It's not easy to spot their positions. They're camouflaged. What can they do?"

"OK, OK," the first one snapped angrily. "You can always find excuses. But meanwhile we're getting the worst of it."

The argument stopped when we heard the noisy voices of the returning soldiers, carrying oranges and bottles of squash. One even held a squawking chicken. They stuffed the goods into one of the cars.

"We're leaving in five minutes!" someone called out from the leading armored car, which sped along the line of trucks. "Everyone load up at once!"

The soldiers clustered together in front of the cars. They were joined by several of the villagers, who waved goodbye warmly.

"Good luck!" came the voices of the women and girls, from the windows of their houses.

"Good luck!" whispered an old farmer who stood next to me,

waving his battered old hat. I returned his greeting. He was the
only person in the whole crowd who paid any attention to me.

The signal was given, and the convoy began moving toward
the mountains. I opened the roof covering once more and
looked out. On both sides of the road stretched green, verdant
orchards and well-tended fields. I couldn't see a soul about.

"We're in enemy territory already," the radio operator
announced. His words sent a slight shudder through my body.
I took a sharper look at the landscape. It looked the same as
the countryside on our side of the border. The hum of a plane
engine sounded far above us. The Piper patrol plane was flying
overhead, its noisy motor chugging away and its squat, clumsy
wings rocking from side to side.

"That Piper! Just a heap of scrap iron!" grumbled one of the
soldiers. "I'm surprised it gets off the ground!"

It went on flying low over us, until it disappeared among the
wadis that cut through the mountains.

"We're getting close to Sha'ar Hagai!" the radio operator
remarked. His thick, hoarse voice sounded faint and indistinct,
as if he was talking to himself. Then he added, in a louder voice
and a more definite tone: "I've got a feeling they're waiting
for us."

"You'll have to close the window just now," the machine
gunner warned me. "They can get you from those damn hills."
I shivered.

"Alright." My eyes were fixed on the heavy machine gun lying
on the floor like a faithful watchdog, sitting with its feet stretched
out in front of it. "I'll close it when we get to the hills."

The hills came closer, and the pounding of my heart made
them jump in front of my eyes. Then I calmed down a little, and
the hills stopped shaking.

"Here's Sha'ar Hagai," my neighbor called out. He pointed to the place with his finger. I stared at the ridges of the hills, which seemed to merge into one another. A café built of yellowish stone stood on the crossroads leading from Jerusalem to Beit Guvrin. The shutters of the café were closed, and there was nobody about. On both sides of the winding road were steep, rocky slopes covered with pine trees. The densely-packed trees were inclined inward, as if they wanted to fall onto the road. A cry of warning echoed in my ears: "No entry!"

The roof covering had to be closed. For the last time, I looked back, at the coastal plain strewn with squares of green and patches of yellow sand, vanishing from sight behind the hills. I had a powerful urge to go back. If only I could go back to the training camp. But it was too late for that. I had to carry on. My worried eyes fixed on the road ahead once more. The narrow mountain pass we were now entering looked like a dark tunnel, long and closed.

I slammed the roof opening shut. It closed with a heavy metallic bang. It was pitch dark inside the car. I stretched out my hand to the shutter next to me and opened it wide. Through it I could see the white stones at the side of the road. They moved toward me. The speed of the armored car increased their blinding glare, as if the lights of thousands of small projectors were sending their rays toward me. My gaze strayed to the side of the road. Almost vertical slopes, strewn with stones, ran down to the edge like breakwaters.

The engine of the armored car groaned heavily, struggling to climb the road, which wound up the steep slope. Its incessant groan grated on my ears like the whine of a drill driving through my skull. I pressed myself against the opening. At that moment it seemed like the only avenue to light and sun and the green young life outside. Inside the car, the heavy iron plates pressed on me, radiating a stifling heat. The choking fumes of the engine seeped inside. I drew them into my nose and throat, coughing and swallowing my spit with difficulty.

The car sped past the water pumping station that stood on the rib of a rocky hill, next to the road. At the entrance to the station was an armored half-track, in front of which stood three British soldiers in black berets. They signaled to the passing trucks, pointing toward the hills.

"They're telling us there's an ambush over there," the driver shouted.

"Don't believe them," the radio operator shouted back. "I wouldn't be surprised if they put a few bullets into us themselves—" He didn't have a chance to finish his sentence, before he was propelled into the air. I, too, was lifted into the air, floating. The sound of a heavy explosion hit me. A blinding streak of lightning covered my eyes. Murky darkness. A blow on my skull. My limbs were squashed.

———————

I came to, stiff all over. My eyes squinted in the darkness. With every flicker of my eyelids, my head ached with pain. A bitter, burning taste, like foul sawdust, filled my mouth with sticky liquid. A crushing pain stabbed through me, clinging obstinately to my head, piercing through my skull. I heard a cracking, long ring in my ears, like banging on a thin tin plate. If only I could go back to the dim half-light, the dazed state from which I had just emerged. But everything was getting clearer.

I could move my arm now, but the movement sent a shudder of pain through my body. I put my hand to my head hesitantly.

But I felt nothing, apart from a slight bump, a burning, stinging lump. I went on feeling for broken bones, but found none. Stretching forward, my hands came across a heap of ammunition boxes. My breathing was cut short by a direct stab of pain, which hit me like a blow to the abdomen. Closing my eyes, I doubled up. When I opened my eyes again I saw pale spots of light on the ceiling, vague, blurred openings in the wall of the armored car. The ceiling lay in front of me, on its side. I closed my eyes and opened them again. But the side wall was still above me. The car had turned over.

Fear. A wave of hot blood rushed to my head. A mad thumping in my heart. Fright. The chatter of a machine gun joined the ringing in my ears, banging away with a distant rattle, like faint voices. The shots came nearer. Their anger gathered like thunder. Machine guns snarling in staccato coughs. Guns barking somewhere, their thin sound almost swallowed in the salvoes of shots from other weapons. Another, lighter sound hovered in the air. Submachine guns. The convoy had run into an ambush. *What about the other cars?* I thought suddenly, panicking.

I lifted myself on an elbow, with great effort. Dizziness. Everything moved and shook. I felt I had to lie down on the floor, to hide. But I fought this oppressive feeling. Thin white smoke floated in a long trail over the pile of objects and boxes of ammunition in front of me. Choked groans and the sound of a man whispering. My heart leaped with joy to hear voices. Signs of life. I turned to one side, trying to get to my knees despite the pain. But I stumbled. I tried once more, and this time I made it.

My eyes fell on a figure lying next to me, a blurred, shadowy figure moving in the wind. I made out his face: a pale face struck by shock. Clenched lips moved, but I heard nothing. A hand came out and touched my shoulders. His face came closer.

I heard some muffled words, slowly, like the sound of an echo among deep valleys. "What's . . . hap . . . pened . . . to . . . you?" I didn't know what to say. I was confused. Stunned. Panic-stricken. Once more I felt my body and shook my head. "Nothing, I don't think anything's . . ." Talking made the ringing in my ears sound louder, like the whistle of a train slowing down. Tears of pain rolled down my cheeks. Crying made me feel more relaxed.

"What about the others?" I stammered in a choked voice.

"Two of them have been hurt. I thought you were too." Now I recognized his wild forelock of straw-colored hair and peaceful blue eyes. It was the soldier who had grumbled about the poor aerial observations.

"They got us, huh?" He nodded his head, pinching his narrow lips in concern.

The bundle next to me moved, and out crawled the radio operator. "The set's smashed," he moaned.

"The accompanying armored cars will reach us soon," the soldier next to me said. "They saw us turn over." I picked myself up and looked through the open window. The shots thundering outside pressed against my ears and my forehead. From time to time the bullets hammered against the wall, which shook as if the steel was going to split. I had never imagined the sound of a shell could be so deafening. My hand, which rested on the wall, sweated, and shook with the vibration of the steel plates. Would I have the strength to lift myself another little bit in order to see what was happening outside?

Slowly I placed my cheek next to the steel wall. Its heat burned the skin on my face. A shell struck the wall near the shutter, and the shock of it threw me back. But I put my face next to the shutter again. Through it I could see a strip of road. At first, I could only make out the thick tires of the trucks.

But I lifted myself up until I could see the trucks themselves. They weren't moving, but their engines were still running. It looked as if the drivers still intended to continue the journey. On the other side of the trucks were the wild rocky slopes and the pine trees. Their closeness was frightening. They were so near, and yet I couldn't see a human form anywhere in the area.

Where was the enemy? Where were the shots coming from?

I couldn't detect any movement. But the shots became heavier. I had a growing feeling that trouble was on the way. We were facing a disaster. I had to get out of there! My eyes wandered around anxiously over the steep slope facing us. The treetops of the pines looked like a heavy cloud. My eyes penetrated it, noticing the small dark spots of the cones. Sunbeams filtered through the branches, winking at one another and changing shadows constantly, like a traffic light at a dangerous corner: "Danger, danger," they said. I looked down at the trunks of the trees. A dark, sinister shadow, like a black and terrifying lake.

The smell of petrol and smoke. The thin smoke had become thick and pungent. The petrol tanks and the boxes of ammunition! They could catch fire. I flung off my jacket and threw it over the tanks and the boxes. Warm sweat trickled over my body. I tried to wipe it, but the feeling of dampness remained.

"Where's your first-aid box?" the driver called out.

"Here," the radio operator answered, holding the box out to him.

"What about the wounded?"

"They need a doctor. We must get them out of here at once." The radio operator added: "We'll all have to leave."

The driver crawled back to the wounded men in the front of the armored car, carrying the first-aid kit. The operator crept cautiously to the back door and opened it. "There's an armored car!" he cried out. "Coming our way!"

The shots were becoming more intense. Someone yelled out to us from the armored car that had just stopped: "Get out of here. Climb into the trench next to the road. Hurry up!"

"The door won't open," the soldier next to the door called nervously. "The hinges are broken!" He began hitting the handle of the lock with the butt of his rifle.

"Don't use force," the driver broke in, coming up behind him. "It'll be alright." He began working away energetically, until the door moved in place with a creak. "I've done it," he announced happily. The smoke burst outside, and the noise of the splattering bullets entered loudly.

"We're going," the driver shouted to the armored car behind us. "But first we'll take the boxes of ammunition into the trench."

"OK," they replied. "But hurry up. We have to pick up some wounded men from the trucks."

We began pushing the boxes toward the door. There the driver rolled them away and placed them in the trench. I turned my head and looked inside the car. The radio operator and machine gunner were dragging the wounded men toward the door.

"Where's the machine gun?" I asked.

"There, next to the wall." The machine gunner motioned toward it with his head.

"I'll take it." Without waiting for an answer, I crawled inside and took it. I looked back. Almost everybody had left the car already, but one man remained.

"Help me get this box out," I said. He took hold of the box and came up to the door. But suddenly he left it, turned around, and went back inside the car.

"What the hell are you doing?" I snapped. "We have to go."

"I'm looking for my chicken," he replied calmly. "My parents will never forgive me if I don't bring it along."

"Chicken?" I exclaimed. "What chicken?" The shots made it hard to hear anything. He made some reply, but I couldn't make out what he said.

"Come back!" I shouted. "Come back at once!"

Sudden silence. For a moment I was able to hear him.

"The chicken I bought in Ekron," he tried to argue. "I'm looking for it . . ."

I lost my temper. "Leave your smelly chicken and jump into the trench." He pretended not to hear me. I turned around angrily and was about to grab him and pull him along. But shouts from the armored car next to us stopped me.

"Jump into the trench," I heard an order, "and wait there. We'll come back later." The car dashed off. My eyes were glued to the windows of the departing car.

"Wait, wait," I shouted. "I'm coming!" But they couldn't hear me. I looked inside and saw the soldier's face beaming with happiness.

"Got it! Got it!" he cried out, waving the white chicken.

"You bloody idiot," I yelled. "They left us behind, all because of that damn fowl." I slammed the door shut.

"It's gone?" He could hardly believe it. "Gone?" He gave me an embarrassed look.

"Yes, it has," I imitated his whining voice. But his shamefaced looked calmed my anger a little. There were only two of us left now, and there wasn't much point in quarreling. We were in quite enough trouble already. Anyway, he looked as if he was about to burst into tears.

"OK, OK," I said, a bit curtly. "Take it easy."

He looked relieved.

"Take your gun," I went on. "We'll open the door and jump into the trench. You can take the chicken along as well," I added in a conciliatory tone. "By the way, what's your name?"

"Yoram," he said. A shy smile spread over his sunburned face. "I really put you in a spot, didn't I?" he remarked apologetically.

"Never mind." I was in a hurry. "Get ready for the jump." I dragged the machine gun to the opening of the door. "Ready?" We kicked the door open and jumped into the trench. The shots sounded clear and sharp, whistling and piercing. Their noise cut through the flesh of my body, peeling my skin, cutting my breath short, ripping my clothes off. Both of us fell into the trench and rolled about among the scattered boxes of ammunition.

I pressed close to the stony ground and hugged it. But my arms seemed to be too short, my grasp too weak. I buried my face against the sharp gravelly soil. I didn't feel it stabbing although it cut deep into my flesh.

Where was the enemy? The bullets stung the ground, and the gravel spattered. Where were they shooting from? I lifted my head carefully. A ridge of steep rocks stretched above me. Rows of rocks, like columns of white tombstones, standing as if they were about to fall, to collapse on top of me.

The shots hammered into my head. I buried it in the little craters in the ground. The sound of explosions banged against my temples, making my head spin. Thoughts pressed against one another, split in half, were cut into ribbons. *Why had I left the armored car?* I was pleased that Yoram was also there. He would help me. He'd know what to do. The others would also help me. The men from the armored car had told us to wait for them in the trench. They would soon come back to collect us. They wouldn't forget. They *couldn't* forget. They had to help us.

We were in trouble. Maybe they thought we could help *them*. But what if Yoram was pinning his hopes on *me*? Ridiculous! Who was I, and what could I do? My hands were trembling. My stomach was shrinking and contracting. I was useless. Utterly useless. I had to get out of there. To get out . . . to run away . . .

I looked toward the road, hopefully. The trucks were in a close-packed line, touching one another, as if they wanted to stick together and form a single mass of iron. Their barred openings were shut tight, and the bullets hammered against them. The steel plates were falling to pieces. But the sides deflected the bullets, with only sparks of fire ricocheting off the rusty metal.

A whistling explosion. A long, deafening thump. *A mine!* I thought at once, burying my head in the ground.

"A tire's burst," Yoram said. He spoke like an expert. "They always shoot at the tires," he added knowingly.

I looked at the row of trucks once more. A big truck had been split in half, and its two halves lay on the dusty road. The shots were aimed at it. Sacks of flour had been strewn all around, raising clouds of whitish dust. Thousands of little fountains of white rose from them into the air of the wadi. An armored car made its way to the shattered truck. It tried to push away the wreckage, which was blocking the road. But it failed.

"It's a damn nuisance!" Yoram whispered anxiously. "If they can't move the broken truck, the road will stay blocked." He held the submachine gun close to his cheek but didn't lose his grip on the chicken, not for a second. He had tied a string around its legs and fastened the other end to his belt.

The firing had died down. I raised my head a little and looked at what was happening on the other side of the road. I could make out a deserted stone building almost hidden by dense trees. The trucks on the road prevented me from seeing the whole area. But I could distinguish a flat plain planted with tall bushes, which formed a bay of green and ran into the hills around the building. That was the place! An idea flashed into my mind. The ruined building looked to me like a better shelter than the exposed trench.

"Listen, Yoram," I said with decision, "what do you think about moving over to the ruin?" The short break in the shooting made it easier for us to decide. "We'll run for it to the other side of the road, and then we'll be OK," I summed up the situation.

Yoram didn't reply. But I noticed that he took a box of ammunition and threw it forcibly to the other side of the road. I did the same with another box. Then we looked at one another and jumped out of the trench, rushing as fast as we could toward the ruined building. A hail of bullets pursued us. We ran, doubled up, between the row of trucks, wherever we could find an opening. The road shuddered with the impact of the bullets. A white mist rose from the asphalt, where the bullets chipped the road. The twenty strides to the building seemed like a long, exhausting, and almost endless journey.

We reached the stone wall and flung ourselves down next to it, surprised to find that we were untouched by the bullets.

CHAPTER 4

THE TRAP

We burst into the ruin and fell to the floor, where we lay exhausted. My breath came back to me slowly. It was half-dark in there. Four massive stone walls covered with lichen closed us in. Through the opening above I could see thick treetops leaning on the roofless walls. *That's good,* I thought to myself, *they'll shelter us.* The shots continued with a biting rattle, but their sting was blunted. The walls were thick. Their strength and protection relaxed us and made us feel secure.

"You see?" I remarked to Yoram.

"Yes, not so bad. Let's take a look outside."

I got up. Through the dense upper branches of the trees the shape of the hill appeared. Thick vegetation—trees, bushes, and tall wild grass—covered its slopes. Pale flashes of fire flickered through the wood, darting through the low stone fence and leaving instantly. The enemy was about two hundred yards away.

I lifted the machine gun excitedly and aimed it at the place where the flickers were coming from. The edge of the fence moved through the front gun sight, more flashes. The blade of the rear sight moved like a compass's arm along the length of the low hill. I waited hungrily for the appearance of another flash, which would show me where to aim. A flicker. My finger pressed the trigger of the machine gun. The fire that poured from the barrel flooded and swallowed the tiny figures coming down from the hill. White dust rose in the air over the fence, a mixture of stone splinters and chips of wood from the branches of the tree. A man straightened up, clasped his chest, stood stoutly, and then sank down. The clasped hands fell to his sides in a rapid, staccato movement, as if they belonged to a mechanical doll whose spring had run down. As the hands fell, they seemed to drag with them the bent-over body, which rolled down the hill between the rocks.

"You got him!" Yoram yelled out happily. I was stunned. Something inside me fluttered and hammered against my chest. Revulsion at what I had done. I pulled away from the butt of the machine gun for a moment. I'd killed him. Why had I done it? A blast of flame blinded me. A volley of shots rang out. I turned to the left, to the road. A truck had burst into flames there and gone up in a blazing pyre. Bright tongues of fire, and the shouts of despairing men. My cheek rested against the butt of the gun once more. My finger pressed the trigger. I fired at the other side of the rocks over the road.

The smell of burning drew my attention to the truck, from which black smoke poured in gusts. Through the suffocating smoke appeared the shape of a man running toward the truck, kicking the door, trying desperately to open it. The shots focused on him. I fired at the rocks once more, until the thick black smoke covered the whole depression and hid it from view.

"There are people in the trench!" Yoram shouted. He took my hand and turned my face toward it. Through the smoke, I saw people lying motionless. "They're firing at them," he added.

A trumpet blast emerged from the burning hollow between

the hills. A wild, prolonged blast. Voices shouting in triumph, and whistles. A cold shudder went through me, as if a cold iron rod was being passed over the joints of all my bones. The attack . . . their attack was starting. The dry crack of submachine guns. Out of the wooded slopes came hundreds of crouching figures. They moved toward the road with short steps and hops, bending down every now and then to hide behind the rocks. Some of them rushed forward, toward the road.

The firing stopped for a moment, and the forward rush halted. But the hostile shouts went on reverberating. "How are you, Mr. Mizrachi?" someone from between the rocks called out in a jeering voice. "Come here, Mr. Mizrachi, and we cut your throat." A chorus of guttural, high-pitched yells, like the howling of jackals in the night, accompanied this taunt. The whistles shrilled, and the trumpet blared again. A muffled, stubborn sound came from afar: dull, thudding sounds at a slow pace. A sort of drumming . . . the sound became clearer, drums. And with them the ringing sound of something striking against tin cans. Thin, delicate sounds. In the background a growing shout that became louder and pierced the air.

"What's that?" I asked anxiously.

Yoram leaned against the wall, his machine gun ready to fire. "They're spurring their soldiers on with tins and drums. That's all." More cries cut into his words like jackals' howls. "Those are the women and children from the nearby villages. They always do this." Now the high-pitched voices stopped yelling and began wailing and lamenting. "Yes," Yoram said, "some of them must have been wounded or killed. They're picking them up now."

The wailing was replaced by cursing and oaths. "Smash their limbs," hundreds of throats shrieked madly in unison.

"Smash them . . . smash them . . . smash them to pieces!"

The drums hammered at fever pitch. Their beat shattered into thousands of echoes in the valley between the hills.

"They're crazy . . . crazy," I whispered faintly.

Yoram moved toward me, and I went closer to him. Our drawing closer quieted a little the shudder that had begun making my knees shake. My hands, which caressed the machine gun, twitched nervously. I clutched the gun butt tightly, and my shuddering stopped. I gave the gun an affectionate look: its black barrel seemed to have grown longer and more powerful—and so had I.

"Mustn't waste bullets," Yoram counseled. "We haven't got very many." I looked at his sweaty face and then at the trench beside the road. The people there were moving toward us. "Must be the drivers of the trucks," Yoram muttered to himself. "Those bloody Arabs will finish us off. A couple weeks ago they cut up eleven of the boys taking the convoy to Har-Tuv."

"Cut up?"

"They managed to separate one armored car from the convoy," he said in a flat voice. "And when all their bullets were gone . . ." He drew his finger across his throat, with an expressive gesture.

"Yoram," I breathed heavily, "do you know what they'll do to us?" The severed heads in the atrocity pictures came back to me vividly.

"Yes," Yoram sighed sadly, "I know." The firing stopped again. The focal point of the battle had moved to the pumping station, about three hundred meters behind us.

"Hope they haven't forgotten about us," I mumbled glumly.

Yoram flashed me an encouraging look. "Don't worry," he said, trying to sound confident. "They won't forget us."

But this only made me more scared. "And if the armored car

gets hit? No one in the rest of the convoy knows we're here . . ." I shook my head vigorously, as if trying to chase away this thought. My hands tightened on the gun, as if gripping it would give me confidence.

The short truce ended abruptly. The machine guns stationed on the hill tattooed the walls of the ruined building again. My whole body went taut, and I peered at the edges of the copse, near the road. A spaced-out row of shapes burst out from it. I fired at them, and they disappeared behind the stones. I threw a quick glance at the trench on the side of the road. The people who lay in it moved toward the ruin, crawling slowly on their hands and knees. They froze the moment the machine guns started firing again. I stared straight ahead of me, over the barrel of my gun.

"They're here," Yoram shouted into my ear. "They're here."

"Who?" I asked, without taking my eyes off the hill.

"The men from the trench. One of them is hurt."

I turned around. Three people were lying in the entrance to the building. Their hands grabbed the earth loosely, and their heads were close to the ground. Two of them had struggled to get to their feet, and remained sitting on their haunches. The third was motionless.

"He's wounded," the oldest of them observed, as if explaining why he didn't move. "In the chest."

I came up to the wounded man and turned him over on his back gingerly. He was about fifty. His large, balding head moved side to side with tiny, cramped motions. He murmured something between his parted lips, but I couldn't make it out. Bubbles of foam sprayed from his mouth. The other two men bent over him. One of them took a handkerchief and wiped away the foam that had dripped onto his chin. "He's badly hurt," he said worriedly. The wounded man's eyes stared somewhere up in the air. I passed my hand in front of his eyes. But he didn't react.

"It's shock," the other man said. "Shock, that's what it is!"

"A truck driver?" Yoram asked.

"Yes, we all are."

"Can you look after him?" I asked uncertainly.

"Yes, I can." The man stopped speaking and sighed. "I was a partisan . . . with the underground. In the forests of Russia. I can look after him."

"What's your name?" Yoram asked with a look of awe.

"Yosef." While replying, he bent over the injured man and wiped the sweat away from his forehead. "Is there any water?"

"No."

This didn't surprise him. He went on treating the wounded man, opening his buttons and taking off his belt.

"Do you have a gun?" I asked Yosef.

"No."

"I suppose you lost it when you dragged him away."

"No, no. I went out without a gun."

"It's quiet out there," the other driver said in his rough voice. He was holding a large Mauser. "What d'you think the chances are?" No one answered. "My name is Berkowitz," he added. "A veteran truck driver, with thousands of miles on the road." He stressed the word "veteran," as if it was a rank or title.

We looked out again at what was happening outside. There were some isolated shots. Sounds of battle also came from the pumping station. "To be a driver in one of these convoys today is as bad as getting typhus," Berkowitz grumbled in his deep voice. "It's alright for you youngsters. No wife, no children, nothing to worry about. But what about me? Just take me." His voice rose nearly to a scream. "A wife and three kids in Tel Aviv. And where am I? Here, damn it, here, in the middle of the fighting!"

"Well, you aren't the only one," Yoram retorted rudely. Berkowitz didn't seem to like this answer, because he snorted angrily. "You young pipsqueaks think you know everything, don't you?"

Yoram ignored him. "What's the time?" he asked me.

I brought my watch up to my eyes. The twisted bundle of wires was smashed to pieces. All the same, I could make out the hour hand, which had stopped at four. About an hour must have gone by since then. "About five," I told Yoram.

"It'll be dark in about an hour," he said, thoughtfully.

Night was approaching, bringing with it a dull feeling of dread. The oppressive shadow of the mountains cut into the winding path of the wadi. I turned around to see where the sun was, but it had disappeared. Its bright light was reduced to a yellow streak, which stretched above the ridges of the mountains like a luminous belt around a narrow strip of heaven and sky. The fresh green of the trees that covered the slopes mingled with the white sheen of the wild rocks. A mosaic of vibrant colors quivered and hung in the air like shimmering butterflies. The objects in the landscape took on the deep colors of strong shadows, until they seemed to have been refined and applied especially for this moment before sunset. A painful feeling of disaster seeped into me. What was all this for? We were going to die!

No, it was impossible, impossible. I didn't believe that I was going to die. Something inside me quivered, squeezing the air out of my chest, emptying it until I felt I was choking. My heart beat strongly. My Adam's apple twitched madly. Cold sweat covered my face. My chin dropped downward with a shuddering weakness. The only things that stayed powerful were my thoughts. They went on flickering through my brain.

I remembered my parents, my mother and my father. Their nearness, even in the mind, gave me some warmth. A feeling of remorse filled me, pangs of conscience for the way I had treated them in the weeks before going out to fight. All they had tried to do was to express their concern for me, and I had been harsh to them. I could still see their confused looks when I scoffed and jeered at their fears about what could happen to me in wartime. "You're always worried," I shouted at them contemptuously. "Always anxious and worried!" They seemed to be typical ghetto Jews, always timid and afraid, whereas I was a real sabra, a Jew born in Israel, who had no time or patience for the weak-kneed Jews from abroad. And although they were my parents, I felt superior to them—almost as if I was not their flesh and blood. And now I was tasting fear, the bitter taste of fright. Now I understood . . . Did I still have a chance? Was there any hope at all?

Night. Night . . . We would escape under cover of darkness. Night. Night . . . I struggled to suck some air into my collapsed lungs. Yes, there was still a chance. Darkness . . . Night. When would it come? I glanced at my broken watch again.

Yosef's words cut into my thoughts. "It's quiet," he whispered, raising himself a little over the wounded man. "Maybe they've gone away?"

"Don't bluff yourself," Yoram interrupted him. "They won't leave here until they've finished us all off." He seemed to enjoy the look of terror on Yosef's face.

"I think," Berkowitz chimed in, "that there's a good chance of our armored cars getting through from Jerusalem. We've been stuck here for a couple of hours already. What are they waiting for? Are they fast asleep? They've had plenty of time to get here." He looked up at us, as if hoping we would confirm what he was saying. "Well, what do you think, children?" he asked.

"Maybe."

"We'll get bugger all," Yoram said, in a loud, protesting voice. "Bugger all, I tell you, let alone armored cars and troops." The shots began again. "See what I mean?" he exclaimed triumphantly. "They're still there." The cries of battle began reverberating once more in the direction of the pumping station. Because it was far away from us, it sounded like the shrill, discordant wailing of angry dogs whose tails were being crushed.

"So, what's going to happen?" Berkowitz cried out in a trembling voice.

"If no reinforcements arrive by nightfall, we'll try to get out of here somehow," Yoram said.

"And what about him?" Yosef asked, pointing to the wounded man. "He can't move."

"We'll drag him along," Yoram said. He nodded at me. "He and I—we'll see he comes along."

"Yes, that's right," I seconded him, in a choked voice.

"And what are the chances of getting through?" Berkowitz persisted.

"So-so," Yoram said.

"Stop playing the fool," I said to Yoram. "Try to be serious for once in your life. You know the area, don't you?"

"Yes, of course," Yoram replied. "There are a lot of things we can do." His voice was a combination of scorn and bitterness. "We can try to escape in the direction of the pumping station." He jerked his eyes in that direction. "But there we'd have a good chance of getting a bullet in the head from one of our own boys. They'll think we are Arabs. That's if we crawl out quietly—and that's what we'll have to do. Because if we make a noise, we'll get a bullet from the Arabs." He stopped for a moment in order to test our reactions. Then he added: "The other possibilities are to try to reach Neve Ilan, about ten kilometers from here, or the coastal plain, which is about thirty kilometers away. That's the position."

"Which way is the safest?"

"I'm not an insurance company."

"And what do you think?" Berkowitz turned to me. He fixed his eyes on me as if I was his last hope.

"Listen, Berkowitz," I answered, feeling uncomfortable, "it's all a question of luck." I wasn't familiar with the area. I could make a shrewd guess, but not be absolutely sure. Berkowitz's face fell, and his head dropped in sadness. I felt sorry for him in his distress. He was probably thinking about his wife and children.

"Very nice indeed," Yosef blurted out, really scared by now. "What sort of an answer is that?"

"Look, boys," Yoram interrupted with a strained smile, "when God wants it, even cows can fly." We all laughed, rather sadly. "Anyway, we'll have to wait and see."

Silence spread dismal wings over all of us. The only sound was the wounded man's subdued groans. Yosef bent over him, lifted his head, and propped it against the wall. I could make out the wounded man's face quite clearly. It was pale. I was shocked by the change in it. The skin of the face had crumpled up and gone as yellow and faded as a piece of old parchment.

"Who knows if he'll even live until tonight?" Yosef broke the gloomy silence. "He's losing a lot of blood."

"You'd better lift his head a little higher," Yoram suggested. "And his feet as well. That way he'll lose less blood."

"How many glasses of blood are there in a man's body?" Yosef asked.

No one answered. I shrugged my shoulders. I used to know the answer, but at that moment all my knowledge of first aid had vanished. My eyes wandered over rocks and tree trunks. Their colors had gone, faded into the worsening light. Everything looked dim and murky. The wounded man's sighs became fainter. He was dying. Would I be saved? A terrible feeling of helplessness took hold of me. My whole frame seemed to have shrunk and shriveled up. All my impressions were being wiped out. My strength had been uprooted, leaving me empty. The stones and sticks I stared at seemed so huge: they became longer and longer the more I gazed. Vague, confused colors . . . depressing grayness . . . And I was nothing—zero—nothing at all . . .

Was I really doomed to die? The lust to exist, to live, burst out of me in a rushing stream, a stream that wanted to crack the skin of my flesh, to strip it off me. My breathing became spasmodic, anger coursed through my blood, in every cell of my body. No, I didn't want to die. To be saved—that was the thing: to be saved.

I raised my eyes pleadingly to the strip of sky above my head. It was so deep and soft. Feathery clouds floated aimlessly in the vast space. Was there a God in heaven? My mother had said she would pray for me, would ask that my life be spared. I could see her eyes in front of me. She always used to pray. She was very religious. My eyes prayed, my whole being cried out: "Save me, rescue me. Save my body from the stabbing knives. Please give me a sign that my prayer has been heard."

The heavens gazed at me, expressionless. The roar of explosions and the wild battle cries sounded in my ears, but nothing else. Was that the answer? So that was what happened when one prayed. I lifted my fists angrily and shook them at the sky. I cursed, cursed until I had no breath left. No, there was no salvation from heaven. The machine gun was the only thing I trusted. I bent down low over it and talked to it, kissing the burning barrel. A salty harshness stung my lips.

"What's wrong with you?" Yoram's voice came to my ears.

"I was just thinking . . . You know."

"Yes," Yoram sighed, "I know." He stopped suddenly, as if the words choked him.

"What's the matter, Yoram?"

"Something terrible will happen to my parents if I'm killed."

"We're all going to be killed."

"Yes, yes, I know." He sounded confused. "I'm an only son, you see, and my mother's very attached to me. Since I've been in the fighting, she's insisted that I write to her at least once a week. Well . . ."

"Well what?" I encouraged him.

"Well, on my last leave I wrote ten letters. I put in routine phrases. You know the kind of thing I mean: 'I feel fine, Ma'; 'it's wonderful here'; 'I'm missing all of you,' and things like that. You know . . ."

"Yes," I murmured, and nodded understandingly.

"I put the letters into envelopes, on which I wrote my parents' address. I gave them all to a friend of mine in Jerusalem and asked him to drop them into the post box for me. One letter a week. This way my mother gets her regular letter from me and she's happy." He buried his face in his hands, with a frightened look appearing in his eyes.

"Well . . ."

"Imagine what will happen if I don't come home. My mother will get an announcement about my having been killed—this will take a couple of days. But then, after she knows about it, the letters will keep arriving, one letter a week. She'll go crazy. She'll go crazy, I tell you."

Yosef butted in: "I don't know who's in a worse position: someone who's left behind a family and relations, or someone who has nobody."

A salvo of shots cut his words short. Leaves and twigs were sliced off by the bullets that whistled between the trees.

"Some of those bastards are impatient," Berkowitz sneered, lowering his head. The shots stopped.

"I'm forty-five now," Yosef went on wearily. "Alone in the country, quite alone. A new immigrant." A shy smile. "I wasn't always alone. I had a family. A wife and a child. A boy . . ." his voice trailed off.

"Yes, yes," Berkowitz sighed loudly, as if he wanted to show that he shared his grief.

"Yes, that's how it is," Yosef repeated sadly. Several distant shots barked away, as if the battle had retreated to the other side of the mountains.

"Go on," Yoram said. "Go on."

"We lived in a village on the Polish-Russian border. Suddenly the war broke out. I remember it like yesterday." A deep sigh broke from his chest, and he went on: "I can remember the roar of the cannons, the hum of the planes, and the whining of the bombs that fell from the air. Oh, I remember it all very well."

"Yes, yes."

"I'm sure you've heard the same kind of thing from hundreds of other people. But when something terrible happens to you, you feel it through your whole body, and it's no comfort to know that the same thing has also happened to someone else. My whole family was wiped out. Nobody left. They weren't taken to the gas chambers. No, they were simply taken to a nearby forest, told to dig pits, and then put in front of machine guns.

"I began to be a partisan. I lived in the forests. Revenge: that's all I wanted. Their blood in return for the blood of my family. That's how things went on until the war was over and we had won. Then came the refugee camps. And I came here." He stopped, and his face clouded over again. He crinkled up his forehead, as if trying to remember something. "I didn't even have a chance to get back on my feet, before another war came along." He gave a nervous laugh, and concluded, in a puzzled tone: "And so here I am, with all of you. And it looks like the end of the story . . ."

The silence came back to the four stone walls. The wounded man was taking short, sharp breaths, which slowly turned into a hissing whistle, like the sound of air bubbles traveling through water. His breathing slowed. Each time he released a painful trickle of air, it sounded like his last breath.

An explosion slammed me up against the wall. "A hand grenade," Yoram warned. The thunder of the grenades followed one another. The power of each explosion shook us about and made the building quake. I felt that my eyes were dancing in their sockets. It was hard to see anything: my vision was getting dimmer. Suddenly the commotion stopped, and the quiet was pierced by a loud cry.

"Jewish dogs," a thick, coarse voice shouted, "come out of there!"

"Bitch and son of a bitch," Yoram shouted back in Arabic, "show your face—and we'll shit on it."

"Come out, come out," the horse voice challenged us. "Hold your hands up and come out, you godless dogs." Cries of wild laughter. Yoram looked at us, as if asking, "What should we do?"

"Carry on cursing them," I urged. "It's lucky they're cursing. We have to play for time."

"OK," Yoram said. Then he raised his voice: "Come here," he jeered. "Come on. We're waiting for you."

"We have time, sons of death. Your end is near."

"You have time? You've got shit!" Yoram replied loudly and with such confidence that even I was tempted to believe him for a moment. "Just now airplanes will come with reinforcements," he taunted them.

"We've killed them all already, cut their throats with knives. Very soon we'll cut your throats too." The tone became ominous, threatening. A whistle blew.

"Cut their throats! Kill them all!" the voices grew louder. The firing on the other side of the pumping station increased again. In my heart I began to fear that part of the convoy had indeed been massacred. But I told myself it couldn't be true. It was impossible. They were just trying to frighten us.

The curses and insults flew back and forth, like a game played between two quick and well-matched opponents. Strange how I felt a new sensation spreading through me. The tops of the trees moved calmly, relaxing me. They seemed to say that everything was going to be alright. Hope. Was this just an illusion?

Time went by. I don't know how much time. The sun set, and only its reddish glow lit up the edge of the sky above the mountains that sloped down to the sea.

"He's dead," Yosef's voice boomed out. These two words cut the thread of my thoughts. They had the effect of an electric shock. I let out a sigh of regret, which also had in it a touch of relief.

We won't have to carry him now, the thought flashed through my mind. But immediately afterward my heart gave a twinge: we would have to carry him. After all, we wouldn't leave him in the hands of the enemy. We wouldn't do a thing like that.

I came close to the dead man. His head hung to one side, and his mouth was wide open. Two rows of white teeth gleamed under his lips. From his frozen face, so drained of vitality, two staring glass eyes gave out an ice-cold glitter. It seemed like a mask, with a look of surprise. Was it a smile? His teeth glistened, and his lips were pulled back to the gums. It couldn't be a smile. Perhaps it was just the teeth creaking, grinding against one another, a movement that had stopped in the middle, while his jaws were about to close.

The jeering cries and the curses continued outside. Machine guns chattered and sniped at the ruin; the bullets made splinters of stone fly in all directions. The women's wailing grew louder. The people's presence hung in the air: you could almost feel the people, although you couldn't see them. The valleys seemed to have been emptied, as if they were ready for an approaching tide of humanity. Already, rows of villagers were starting to push their way through to Sha'ar Hagai, moving with irritating slowness, as if they were not in any hurry.

Suddenly a movement pierced the air. A landslide of stones rolling down the slopes. A dark mass burst out from the middle of the wood. A volley of shots, and a donkey came forward. The noise grew louder. At first, I thought these were yells announcing that the attack had begun. But when the donkey knelt down and fell to the ground, I knew that they were the cries of the owner. The injured beast fell onto its back, its four legs waving in the air. They moved, shuddering, in the death agony. Moans of lament and sorrow rose from the mouths of the women in the copse.

"What are they shouting so much for?" I asked.

"For them the donkey means a lot'" Berkowitz answered. "Those bastards took their donkeys along with them to pick up the loot from the convoy." The movements of the donkey's feet grew slower and slower, until they crossed over one another and sank onto its white belly. The animal turned on its side and soon stopped moving altogether.

"Kill them. Kill them," the women shrieked. "Cut them, cut

them to ribbons." The empty tin cans rattled once more, and the drums banged wildly.

A flame flickered toward us. Salvoes of shots increased, swelled, swallowing the thunder of the guns. The voices of people sounded in our ears, not far away.

Cries of insanity? Perhaps I was mad myself? In front of the barrel of my gun, blinding flames danced. I could hardly see anything. Screaming. Shudders . . . smoke . . .

I went on firing madly, feverishly, in a semi-dazed state. Strangely enough, I was able to distinguish the objects within my range of vision. They looked so different. White roses of fire appeared among the rocks, lighting up the surroundings. Their bright leaves spread open quickly and sprayed out to all sides with a loud, sharp explosion. Whitish smoke, light clouds hovering over the earth. The figures galloping forward fell like sheaves before the reaper. Flowers of fire popped up, and new ones bloomed everywhere—a shivering, blazing garden, filled with blinding blossoms. And the more their number grew, the more the wail of the attack increased, until it became a scream. A scream of terror.

"Reinforcements! Reinforcements! Mortars!"

I went on firing furiously. The wave of attacks retreated and was swallowed up in the dark wood. Explosives echoed the rasping sound of the armored cars' motors. The rattling of the submachine guns, whose sound was so quiet, like sunflower seeds being cracked. My eyes were alternately clouded over and cleared. I felt a hand touching my shoulders, and turned around. An unfamiliar face moved in front of me.

"We're from the armored cars . . . the reinforcements!"

The voice rushed at me like a waterfall. A murky whirlpool surrounded me, then settled down and became clear. My eyes

froze in their sockets. On the wall in front of me I made out
Yosef's hunched-up figure. He was crouched over his knees,
curled up and leaning against the wall. A pool of blood lay on the
floor, like a dark stain. Hidden fear fixed my gaze on the pool,
but I lifted my eyes slowly and saw his hanging head. Streams of
blood ran down his face like purple streamers. The top of his
head was missing, as if it had been cut off by a knife. I raised my
hands toward him, mumbling something or other. The soldier
who stood behind me caught my hand.

"You're wounded," he said.

"Wounded? No, I'm not."

"We'll look after you. You've been hit in the leg. But it's not
too bad."

"What d'ya mean, my leg? I was standing behind the wall!"

"Maybe a bullet ricocheted. Or some shrapnel. Does it hurt?"

"Stop talking rubbish. I'm not hurt." The soldier stared at me
in surprise.

"I'm not wounded, I'm telling you!" I insisted helplessly.

The soldier put his arms around my waist and tried to pull me
away. "Come with us," I heard him say. I walked to the armored
car, with him supporting me.

"Maybe we should give him a shot of morphine?" one of the
men behind me suggested. "Do you need an injection?" I didn't
answer. The soldier rolled up my sleeve, without waiting for a
reply, and stuck a needle into my flesh.

Everything became cloudy. Waves rolled, thin strips of bril-
liant colors moved in front of me and merged into my body in
a constant stream, whose touch was soft and pleasant. A pump
ticked away in my head with a soothing, regular sound, which
grew in volume, sucking up into it every noise and rustle from
outside. It beat against my blood in waves, cold and hot waves

. . . cold and hot . . . The pleasant waves stroked the walls of my arteries gently. Their pace quickened until it became so fast that it made my head reel. Cold changed to hot. I could feel every artery and vein in my body. They all beat at an enjoyable pace, like silken streams. My head moved, my heart moved, my blood moved in this enchanted place. Cold-hot, right-left. Cold-hot, right-left. Slumber overtook me, although I didn't want to sleep.

These feelings went on until I woke up.

CHAPTER 5

THE ROAD TO JERUSALEM

A giant lamp hung above my dazed head, in a white circle. Something showed dimly through the icicles of light. A sort of curtain flapped about. Its shining folds contracted and came together, forming the shape of a man bending over me. I blinked my eyes in the strong light. A blurred, hazy face lurched at me from the white circle.

"We've stitched your wounds." A voice fell on me, and the words roused me. Where was I? A pungent smell penetrated my nostrils.

I was lying on a narrow, high bed. My foot seemed to have become longer. My right trouser-leg was cut right up to the groin. The white, blood-soaked bandage that enveloped my calf showed through the torn cloth. I was in a hospital! The man in the white coat was a doctor. I couldn't see very much, but when I looked up I saw hands wearing rubber gloves. Yes, a doctor. Once again, I heard his calm voice: "We've taken a bullet out of your knee." A pause. "The wound isn't serious. You can go back to your unit today. They'll look after you."

My unit? What unit did I belong to? . . . Yes, I remembered. I had to report to the infantry corps headquarters in Jerusalem.

But my leg was pinching me. Its weight pressed on me. But I felt no pain. My thigh was hard as a rock. I could feel clearly the pressure of the envelope of frozen flesh that gripped my thigh bone so firmly.

"What about the leg?" I muttered.

"It's alright. You've got nothing to worry about."

I rose to a sitting position slowly, lowering my leg to the floor as gingerly as I could. I felt dizzy.

"You can walk on the injured leg," the doctor encouraged me. "Don't be afraid. Put weight on it!" He held out his hand to help me.

I touched the floor and remained standing, terrified by the feeling of paralysis that turned my thigh into a foreign body. I was sure some hidden pain was lurking somewhere, waiting, and that any moment now it would attack my injured leg. I didn't actually feel any pain, but my mind told me that my leg must hurt. It was obvious it was going to hurt. So I was all tensed up for the moment in which the current of pain would flow through me.

"Perhaps I can stay here until tomorrow?" I suggested hesitantly. The darkness outside, my weak state, and the dizziness all combined to give me a feeling of insecurity. The idea of going out into a strange town terrified me.

"Sorry," the doctor replied. His encouraging look focused on me. "The hospital is jammed to the rafters. We only take urgent cases. And you'll be alright now."

He put his hand on my calf and ran his palm over the bandage, as if he was feeling a slab of cheese. "In another week, you'll forget you were ever injured," he added.

"But all the same . . ." I tried to go on.

The doctor patted me on the shoulder, and his eyes fixed on me with a determined expression. "We've sent cases much worse than you back to their units. You can get along without us. There's a truck outside, part of the convoy. Get in it and go wherever you have to."

I looked downward. Perhaps they would let me stay here that night, all the same. I stole a look at the doctor. He still looked determined. I had to go. Tears of humiliation welled up in the corners of my eyes. I went out of the ward with slow steps, feeling my way. At first I leaned one hand against the wall, in order to balance myself. But with every step I took I realized that I could put weight on my foot without feeling anything. I went on walking, carefully and hesitantly—but at least I *was* walking. It was bitterly cold outside. My thinly-clad body was exposed to the stinging teeth of the night chill. I had left my coat in the ruined building. I went on walking toward the gate.

There was a group of people leaning against the small truck parked by the curb. "Are you from the convoy?" one of them asked, coming up to me and waving a large notebook.

"No, and yes," I answered in a depressed voice.

"What do you mean?"

"I was assigned to the convoy so I could get to Jerusalem."

"Aha!" the fellow exclaimed, as if he understood what I was talking about. "And in which armored car were you?"

"The first."

"Anyone else with you? Drafted soldiers, I mean—like you. Not regular ones from the convoy."

"No. Why?"

"We want to see if anyone's missing."

"Good. And now maybe you can take me to the Building of the Pillars. That's where my unit is."

"Are you wounded?" asked the tall fellow who stood to one side. He sounded worried.

"Yes."

"I see you're not dressed warmly enough." He took off his heavy army coat. "Take this," he said. "You need it."

"No, thanks," I protested.

"Take it, don't be silly," he pleaded, and without waiting for my reply he put the coat over my shoulders. "You can return it to me tomorrow afternoon," he added. "My name is Eldad. I'll be in the cooperative restaurant."

"Thanks," I blurted out, overcome with emotion. A vague fear gripped me. A feeling of faintness, of unreality. All alone in the cold Jerusalem night. Frozen, despite the coat.

"Come inside," called the driver, who had entered the truck cab. "We'll rush you off to your unit."

I sank into my seat, worn out and exhausted.

The truck set off on its way. Through the windows of the speeding vehicle, I could see dark streets.

"Here we are." The driver's voice woke me from the numbness into which my senses had fallen. "This is the place."

A dark, tall building stuck out of the darkness like a gray mass of marble. I thanked the driver and hobbled to the gate of the building. Two sentries, in long coats and woolen caps pulled down to their eyes, stopped me.

"Where to?"

"I'm looking for Erez, the section commander." I was impatient. I felt that I was going to collapse with weakness and fatigue in another minute.

The sentries gave me a searching look. One of them pointed to the entrance. "Second floor."

With faltering steps I climbed the stairs. There were so many of them, so steep and winding. My calves began to ache. A pulsating current passed through my flesh. It grew more intense, and the frozen feeling began to thaw. A piercing warmth flooded through me. *Now, it's beginning,* a thought flashed into my mind, feeling the pain spreading and drowning me.

When I reached the corridor, I found myself standing in front of a partly opened door. Light. The voices of people behind the door. I stopped a moment to prepare to make an entrance that would make as good an impression as possible. My torn clothes, filthy with blood and mud, made me feel uncomfortable. I caught snatches of conversation. Who could the people be? I heard a voice that sounded familiar. I listened more intently. I realized, to my surprise, that it was the adjutant of the company in Tel Aviv! I'd seen him at the Sarona base only the day before. What was he doing in Jerusalem?

I knocked on the door and pushed myself into the room with dragging steps. Two pairs of surprised eyes pierced into me. I would gladly have turned and bolted, but my weakness fixed me to the spot.

"Shalom," I managed to get out. The two men nodded.

"What happened to you?" the aide asked. He adopted a tone of great anxiety, and even in my depressed state, I could feel it wasn't sincere.

"I caught it . . . in the convoy."

"Sit down, sit down," he invited me, bringing his chair closer. "How do you feel?" I didn't care for the artificial tone.

"So-so. I was wounded a bit."

They nodded.

"I need a bed," I went on, feeling the pain rising in my thigh. "I lost my clothes on the way, and I need new ones."

The adjutant stiffened up. "What do you mean, you lost your clothes?" he asked suspiciously.

"I told you, I lost them in the convoy."

"They may have been picked up and kept in one of the cars," he said, as if trying to convince himself that they weren't really lost. What a subject to bring up at a time like this! "What actually happened there?" he went on.

The expression on my face made it clear I wasn't keen to answer him.

"Leave him alone," Erez interrupted. "Can't you see he's out on his feet?"

"We'll talk about it tomorrow," the adjutant persisted.

"There's nothing to talk about." I was really angry now. "If you want to find anything out, go to Sha'ar Hagai. Maybe you'll find a pair of underpants there."

"I wasn't referring to clothes," he tried to justify himself.

"In a moment I'll fix you up with a bed," Erez interrupted again. "And in the morning you'll get some clothes." He threw the adjutant a furious glance.

"Alright . . . OK," the adjutant grunted in a more conciliatory tone. He stared at me with his tiny eyes, which darted from side to side. *What did this monkey want with me?* I wondered to myself.

"Really, the best thing would be if you went to rest . . . to sleep. You'll feel better tomorrow."

"Good," I answered curtly and in a hostile tone.

"Now I'm going to town," the adjutant mumbled to himself, as if summing up his plans aloud. "Bye, fellows." He waved goodbye and left the room with short, rapid strides, without waiting for a reply. There was something irritating about his appearance. His clothes were carefully ironed, and the collar of his jacket was raised high in a belligerent fashion.

"Come, I'll show you your room," Erez smiled, stretching his hands out to the sides, as if saying, "What can I do when I have to deal with types like that?" I nodded my head in silent agreement.

"Do you need some help?" he asked, glancing at my bandaged leg.

"No, it's alright." I smiled back.

We walked along the long corridor slowly until we stopped beside the door of one of the rooms. Erez opened it. "Come inside." I followed him. He groped around on the wall until he found the light switch and turned it on. A wooden folding bed stood next to a large window, the glass covered with blackout paper.

"I'll make it up for you," Erez said. He went over to the bed and placed on it the folded blankets from one of the cupboards. "How many do you want?" he asked. "It gets cold here at night."

"Four . . . or five."

"Well, it's all ready for you," he declared, straightening up and stretching his back a little. "You can lie down if you like." I walked over to the bed and collapsed on it. I stretched my hand out to the blankets and pulled them to me.

"Wait a moment," Erez stopped me. "I'll take your shoes off for you. It's tiring to sleep with them on." He bent over my feet and took my shoes off. A sharp pain shot through my calf. A damp dizziness spun my head around.

"I'll put the light out . . ." His voice sounded broken, as if it was filtering through to me from a great distance.

"Right . . ." I mumbled softly. Circles spun around at a dizzy pace. Tongues of white and black light galloped after one another in a furious dance. Circle chased circle. Everything went misty in front of me. Blurred . . . everything was blurred . . . I heard dull, muffled rifle shots, frozen, without an echo. The shouts of the attacking Arabs still rang in my head. Was I still there? In the ruined building? In the mountain pass? Cries

of battle. The chattering voice of the armored cars' engines. A
heavy, confused sleep seized me.

I woke up the next day. My eyes opened with a shock. The
objects in front of me looked heavy and squat, as if their propor-
tions had been distorted and their shapes had changed. There
was a bitter, foul taste in my mouth, like the taste of rotten fruit.
I felt a heavy pressure in my throat, and my stomach rumbled,
trying to throw itself onto the edge of my furred tongue. I
wanted to vomit. A burning, stifling mess rose in my throat, but
I couldn't expel it.

A stabbing pain jabbed at the top of my head. I passed my
hand over my skull. My fingers encountered a swelling. I drew
my hand away in fright. Where was I? A pain in my calf reminded
me of the events of the day before. The convoy. I could feel
the burning sensation in my hands and feet, where they had
been stung by crawling on the stones of the road, in the ruined
building . . . the ruined building . . . My eyes were shut, but they
came open again, almost of their own accord. Faint, dim rays.
The sun's light crept into the room. At first it bothered me, but
I soon got used to it, and the objects around me began to return
to their usual shapes. I turned slowly from one side to the other,
trying to find out whether I was still in one piece.

Gradually I pulled the blankets away. I sat up in bed, everything spun around . . . a bandage was wrapped around my calf. A
dark blood stain was sticking to it. Its color looked muddy black.
I wondered whether it was in fact blood. Carefully I touched the
edges of the stain. A warm mildew. Intense stabs of pain, which
ran along my leg, forced me to stop touching it. *It'll pass,* I tried
to encourage myself.

Next to the bed, on a low stool, lay a bundle of clothes. I put
out my hand to pick them up. *This Erez is a fine fellow,* I thought.

After I had dressed, I went to his room. He was standing in the doorway, talking enthusiastically to two soldiers. When he noticed me he turned his head toward me. "Well, how do you feel?"

"Better, thanks." I tried to force a smile.

"Like a cup of tea?" he asked. I muttered a gruff acceptance. "Sit down," he added gently. He put his hand on my shoulder and led me to a chair. "Make some tea," Erez ordered one of the soldiers, who went out at once. "We drink our tea with saccharine." He went on apologetically, "There's no sugar."

"Never mind, it doesn't matter."

The soldier who remained standing next to me gave me an inquiring look.

"You really came off lucky," Erez went on. "Does it hurt very much?" His look showed genuine worry and concern.

"It's not so bad. I can take it."

A faint smile hid itself at the ends of his narrow lips, as if my reply encouraged him. *I'm sure he has enough headaches,* crossed my mind.

"Maybe you should see a doctor," he remarked.

"Perhaps . . . we'll see . . ." An embarrassed silence prevailed for a moment. I inspected his pale face closely. He was short and wiry, and his close-set black eyes looked at me hesitantly, as if saying, "Leave me alone and don't bother me."

The way he fixed the adjutant was just right, I thought. At that moment I had a great affection for him because of this.

"What's the time, Erez?" I asked, trying to get the conversation going. He gazed at his wristwatch again, concentrating hard, as if he found it difficult to read the numbers.

"Eleven," he pronounced eventually, after bringing his scrawny arm right up to his face.

"So late?"

"You really had forty winks last night" the soldier chimed in. He hadn't taken his eyes off me. I smiled at him, as if agreeing, and he replied with a smile.

"Where's the adjutant?" I inquired.

"He'll be back in the afternoon," Erez said contemptuously. "He's going around the town. Showing off . . ."

"Especially to the girls," the soldier chimed in again. He twisted up his face, as if dismissing the whole thing.

"I can't stand him." The two of them laughed.

"Just a *schvitzer*, a braggart," Erez summed up.

The soldier who had gone out returned. "Here," he said, handing me a steaming aluminum cup. I took it from him, and bringing it carefully up to my lips, I began sipping from it.

"Why don't you just stay in bed today?" Erez suggested. "Rest a little."

I looked up at him. "No," I replied. "Feeling better . . . I'll go to town . . . How do I get to the cooperative restaurant?"

"We'll drive you there."

"Alright. Just let me finish my tea."

After I'd finished, we went outside. Erez opened the door of the truck. "Get in," he said. I sat next to him, and we set off. Through the window the streets of Jerusalem looked depressing and disappointing. People threaded their way along the narrow pavement in front of the old stone houses that fronted the street. What had I expected to see? Erez's voice broke into my thoughts: "After lunch . . . We'll meet after lunch." The truck stopped, and I took the coat I had brought along with me and went off to the restaurant.

The woman who sat next to the cash desk, at the entrance, gave me a puzzled look. She was probably surprised to see a customer come so early. "Meals won't be served for another hour," she told me, in a marked Russian accent and a soft voice.

"Never mind. I'll wait."

"Certainly, if you want to." She held out a punched slip. I took it and went into the large, square room. My gaze passed over square wooden tables crowded inside. For some reason they reminded me of the dining room in my school. They used to give us something light to eat at ten in the morning, and the children used to rush inside to get a place as close to the serving counter as possible. In the long run, I chose a place next to the door. It didn't take long before the first of the customers began arriving. Later on, I spotted Eldad's powerful frame. He had a rocking sort of walk, as if he spread his legs out too much. I waved, and he noticed my gesture, although he didn't recognize me right away.

"Do you mean me?" he asked in a slow voice. I looked at him happily.

"Eldad," I called out, "don't you remember me? Yesterday, in the convoy." His eyes lit up, and he slapped his forehead.

"Of course, of course. Well, how are you feeling?"

"Not bad, thanks." He came closer and put his hand on my shoulder. A strong, heavy hand.

"Well, you got off scot-free," he boomed. "You're a lucky bastard."

"I've brought back your coat," I stammered, for lack of anything else to say. "Thanks very much. It was really nice of you."

"Rubbish!" he called out, raising his voice. He shrugged and pulled a face as if he was saying, "It's really nothing, nothing at all." I held the coat out to him. He took it, giving me a broad, happy smile.

"Maybe you'd like to sit down," I suggested. He joined me and threw the coat on the next chair with a careless gesture. "You see," I remarked, lowering my eyes to my new clothes as if showing them off, "I've got new clothes."

"Terrific," he approved.

"And what about you?" I asked. "Are you still with the convoy?"

He wrinkled up his face. "The road to Tel Aviv has been blocked, blown up. Didn't you see it in the paper?"

"No."

"Well, they've really buggered us up this time. It'll take some time before the convoy can get through." He stopped for a moment, looking depressed. "People say Arabs have Nazi experts who volunteered to help them. These explosions may be their work," he added.

"We also have volunteers from abroad."

"Yes," he agreed, "but they're Jews. It's their war too."

"Don't worry," I declared with false enthusiasm. "We'll teach them a lesson they won't forget." But he didn't share my enthusiasm. "You'll see, it'll all be fine," I added, with less confidence.

He smiled sadly. "Got a big job tomorrow, we have. A big convoy has to break through the road. Lots of armored cars."

"Where to?" I asked curiously.

"All sorts of rumors flying about. Still a military secret. Some say to the Etzion Bloc of settlements. It's been cut off for over a month. No supplies can get there."

"I'm sure it'll all be OK."

"I don't feel so good about this convoy," Eldad said sadly. "Not like I felt once, when we used to love doing jobs like this. Today they're making mincemeat of us." He clenched his lips. I could see his teeth cutting into his flesh. He looked worried. Dark patches clustered under his eyes and on his forehead, like distant clouds coming closer across the horizon. I felt how depressed he was. Eldad seemed to read my thoughts. He smiled, trying to encourage me, as if he wanted to say: "Actually, I was just talking nonsense." But I knew this wasn't the case. I could see on his face what he really felt.

"I'm sure this convoy will go to the Etzion Bloc," he murmured, waiting to hear what I thought. I didn't respond. "You know," he said, when he saw I wasn't answering, "the Hebron Arabs are the dregs of humanity. When they can get their dirty hands on one of us, they cut him to pieces."

"Have you seen it yourself?" I asked anxiously. But he didn't seem to have heard my question.

"Hebron . . . a cursed city," he hissed between his teeth, "a cursed place."

"When are you leaving?"

"Don't know. Maybe tomorrow, maybe the day after."

"I'd like to see you again."

He smiled. "If I come back . . ." His voice faltered, but steadied itself at once. "You can meet me here, in this restaurant. You can leave a note with the woman at the cash desk." His greenish eyes clouded over a little, a hint of embarrassment making him lower them, obviously ashamed of what he had said. He seemed to regret saying "If I come back," as if a soldier shouldn't use such dramatic language.

"I'm sure I'll meet you here. I'm quite sure," I added, as if trying to encourage him. I didn't really believe I would ever see him again, and I couldn't deceive him. He read my thoughts and knew I was lying. And he appreciated this.

"You know," he said quietly, running his hand over the pocket of his coat, "I have a spare woolen scarf . . . I don't need it. Take it as a present."

"What for?" I blurted out, surprised.

"Never mind. Take it . . ." He pushed the scarf into my hand. "You need it, and I have another one," he added, trying to make it easier for me to accept the gift.

"Thanks very much," I said, moved by his gesture. "You're really a good fellow." He blushed a little.

"Well, it's time to go. I've got to be in camp." We both rose. "Until we meet again," he said in a flat voice, giving a little smile. A guy who's ashamed of using too many words, it struck me. He was embarrassed by the idea of an emotional parting, just as I was.

"Good luck," I replied. We strolled together through the restaurant, until we came to the street and shook hands warmly. He walked with a heavy, bear-like tread to the armored car at the corner. Before getting inside he turned around and waved to me again. *He walked like a sailor,* I thought, wondering what he had done before the war. I waved back and walked on.

I spent the next two days getting my strength back and taking things easy. On the third day, I was reassigned. "You're being transferred to the outposts in the south of Jerusalem," the adjutant told me. "You must report there tomorrow morning, to the company commander. An armored car will take you there." I nodded to show that I understood, but said nothing. He gave me a quick, furtive look. "Well, that's all."

I presented myself next day before the company commander. His tired face showed indifference, which infected me as well for a moment. "What's your name?" he asked. Then, after I had given it, he asked again: "What did you say?" He cupped his hand around his ear and leaned toward me. I repeated my name. "What? What's that?" the commander stammered in confusion. I raised my voice and pronounced each syllable slowly and with deliberate emphasis.

"Oh, yes," he said finally, as if he understood. "We are waiting here for reinforcements to arrive. Are you a section commander?" I nodded. "When they get here," he went on, "settle down and entrench yourself in the southern outpost." He pointed to the place. "Until then you'll remain here in the company headquarters. I'll see that one of the men shows you the lay of the land. He paused and gave me a friendly look. "How old are you?" he asked.

"Eighteen."

"Yes." He didn't seem to have heard me. "The reinforcements should have reached us today. They were probably held up because of the convoy . . ."

"What convoy?"

"The one that came back from the Etzion Bloc and got stuck in the hills near Bethlehem, not very far from here." He turned toward the range of hills to the south of Jerusalem. "You can see the place from here."

"What's the situation out there?"

"Lousy. They're completely cut off and encircled." He saw the expression of concern on my face. "We're negotiating through the Red Cross to get them out of there," he added. My eyes remained fixed on the ridge of hills to which he had pointed. I could feel their cool dampness, the dampness of a deep cellar. I hated those far-off hills, the dark, sinister peaks that reached into the edges of heaven like the sharp teeth of a rusty saw. *He knew it would happen,* I thought, conjuring Eldad's sad face. I also knew it was going to happen. We both felt it—"it," a vague, unexplained word intended to express the worst, something one could not put into words.

"You'd better arrange a place for yourself to sleep," the commander suggested. He added, "Life has to go on, you know."

"What's the time?" He didn't hear my question. It occurred to me that there was something wrong with his hearing. "Right," I said. "I'll fix it up now."

"Talk to the sergeant. She'll show you your room," he

concluded our talk. "She's in the room next door."

I turned to the sergeant's room and knocked on the door.

"Yes, what is it?" she asked in a high-pitched voice.

As I went in, she lifted her black-haired head. Thick-rimmed glasses bestrode her nose. I gave her a curious look. Her whitish face was covered with tiny acne spots. She moved around in her seat restlessly. My eyes fell on the army sweater she wore tightly around her body. Under it were two sagging breasts, which hung loosely, like two empty sacks of flour. *Too bad she isn't more attractive,* I thought to myself.

"Well?" she asked coldly.

"The commander said you'd give me somewhere to sleep."

She looked me over from head to foot. "That's not a problem," she said in a brisk, efficient voice. "You can stay in the platoon commander's room. His name is Yoska, and it's in the building opposite."

"And where's Yoska?"

"In the hospital. A sniper got him."

"Oh . . . I hope it's not catching."

She laughed. I went outside with her to the yard. I noticed the stooped figure of the company commander, hurrying toward the building.

"He's a terrific fellow," she said with real feeling in her voice. We remained standing there in silence until the company commander reached us.

"It's all over," he told us sadly. "We've just had a wireless message . . ."

"I knew it . . ." The words escaped me. He stared at me in astonishment.

"What do you mean?" he asked. I didn't reply. "Yes," he continued, as if remembering a detail he had forgotten. "You just go to the arms room and take a gun." He gave me a strange look and hastened on to the building.

After carrying out his orders, I went to my room. Through the window, I could see the hills of Hebron. An ominous feeling coursed through me, as if storm clouds were gathering on the horizon far, far away. Would something happen to me as well? I clutched the rifle firmly, intimately. A murderous desire pulsed wildly in my blood. I longed to shoot—to shoot and to destroy. I knew then that the metal weapon was part of me, part of my body. An inseparable part of me.

CHAPTER 6

SIGHT

The next day the weather was pleasant. The winter sun slanted over the barren hills of Judea, scattering its caressing rays generously. The trees and bushes stretched their branches upward in a relaxed way, trying to catch and absorb every shred of warmth. The damp earth and chilly rocks seemed to be stretching themselves out and throwing off the bleakness of winter.

"On days like these, visibility is good and you've got to watch out for snipers," the section commander, Ilan, warned me. We were making a reconnaissance tour of the area, and he was showing me the way to the outpost. "They fire from the heights on the other side of the valley." The stone-strewn terrain that stretched in front of the dense forest did not look like a place from which danger threatened. "The sniping comes from the edge of the forest," Ilan added, as if he had read my thoughts. He pointed toward the domed hill with a beefy hand.

"You've got a nice pair of field glasses," I interrupted, changing the subject and looking at the glasses that hung over his shoulder.

"Yes, they're really first-class." He patted them affectionately. "I got them as a present from an old friend of the family. We live in the same neighborhood, not far from the Tel Aviv seashore. They date back to World War I."

"The First World War?"

"Yes, they're ancient. The friend who gave them to me was once the commander of a warship in the German Navy. When the Nazis came to power, he left and came here. I was given the field glasses when I was ten."

"How old are you now?"

"Eighteen."

"Just like me."

He looked at me as if estimating my age, and then said: "You look younger."

"You're right. And it annoys me. People think I'm still a child."

"And how old do I look to you?" He fixed me with his clear eyes.

"At least twenty."

"That's because I have a broad skull. It makes you look older."

"Yes," I said, "and you have an athletic body."

A happy smile spread over his full face. "Actually, I'm not much of a sportsman."

"Then you must have done a lot of physical work," I tried again. He smiled and shook his head.

"Guess again," he prodded me. "If you can't get it this time, I'll tell you myself."

"Right," I agreed. "But first finish your story about your neighbor."

"Where was I?"

"You were saying that you got the field glasses when you were ten."

"That's right . . . Well, every morning he used to go out on the porch and look at the sea through his field glasses. Probably felt like a captain. He noticed me looking at the glasses with such longing day after day. And when I turned ten, he gave them to me. When he put them in my hand, he sighed and muttered to himself: 'For me it's all over.' Maybe he imagined all the time that he was really on the bridge of his old ship, and when he parted with the field glasses, he also parted from his dream."

While we were talking, we came to an arch made out of concrete pillars. Several neglected stone houses were scattered on the other side of it.

"From now on keep your head down," Ilan said in a serious tone. "Over there is an enemy machine gunner who fires on the dining room." He didn't give me a chance to ask any questions before he sprang from his place quickly and ran toward the door of the building. I sprinted after him. A salvo of shots boomed out with a sharp explosive sound, like a series of hammer blows that shattered the clear glass of the frozen air. Chips of stone, enveloped in thin dust, spattered over me. I ran quickly and leaped into the opening of a sandbagged position at the entrance to the dining room.

"Not bad for a start," Ilan jeered. I called out a few words to him, which were swallowed up in my short, quick breathing. About three hundred meters away was an exposed stone hill, shaped like a banana, whose dome faced our direction. Beds of stone dotted its slopes with thousands of white spots, like mushrooms that had come out on the face of the slopes that stretched down in steps to the valley below. A low stone building in the center of the hill was the only thing there that wasn't carved by nature.

"Where are they shooting from?" I asked, after I had tried but failed to discover signs of human beings in the area.

"From the building."

"Those machine gunners are real bastards," I snorted. "To fire at three hundred meters with a machine gun—and still miss!"

"Don't ask for trouble," Ilan picked me out. "You'll annoy them."

"Well, shall we continue on to the position on the slope?" he asked, as if trying to find some sign of hesitation on my part.

"Why not? After all, we have to get there. Isn't that so?"

We began running toward the buildings on the slope, until we flung ourselves inside a foxhole dug on the side of the hill. Several soldiers lay on blankets spread out on the ground. They gave us a casual look. "Maybe you'll stop walking on our blankets?" one of them complained.

"Move aside, and stop telling me what to do," Ilan reprimanded him. But no one answered. I peered out of the foxhole. The eastern part of the battle front stretched along its whole length.

The white mountain peaks looked like the tops of mosques. A wall along whose ridges blue mist crept, trying to climb up to its lofty peaks. In the middle stood a chain of low hills that ran southward, like a low barrier. It looked like a row of extinct volcanoes. Unlike a wall of great mountains, this barrier was open and cut through by ravines, which began with broad breaches of the hills and continued in narrow corridors that wound down steeply to the gaping abyss that stretched down to hollow and ominous horizons.

"From here you can see the Dead Sea," Ilan explained, following my glance. The sea looked like a long, narrow stain, or like a dark blue cloud that had sunk between the yellow slopes of the mountains.

"Let me have a look," I said. He held the field glasses out to me. I brought them close to my eyes. Through the glasses the ravines that dropped down toward the Dead Sea looked even deeper. Now I could feel sharply the emptiness that hovered in the intervening space.

On the right a verdant valley stretched out. Low stone fences crisscrossed it, making it look like an inlaid checkerboard. A long, low hill shaped like a finger stuck out into the valley, as if it wanted to stop the valley from sweeping it up and into the deep ravines behind it. At the end of this finger, near the place where the nail would be, lay the enemy village. It was hard to see it: its houses, built of natural stone from the surrounding hills, merged and blended with the colors of the earth.

"Now I'll show you the other parts of the front." Ilan smiled good-naturedly. "We'll have to run all the way again," he summed up.

We hopped and leaped between the trees and the buildings on the slopes. When I rose up, I felt even more vividly the depth of the ravines that surrounded the hill. I was slightly giddy, as if I stood on the brink of a deep chasm. The snipers! A hair-raising shudder passed through me. I got gooseflesh. I felt thousands of frozen needles pass over my body. There was a salty feeling in my eyes. It was hard to breathe. Every step was torture. We reached the gate, exhausted and sweating. From there we went on marching through the open field, toward the other side of the front. I stopped for a moment and asked Ilan to lend me his field glasses again. Through the lenses my eyes moved over the high plateau of the Hebron mountains, which stretched to the east and linked up with the sandy-peaked mountains and chalk cliffs of the Judean desert. My gaze returned to the ravine that sprawled out in front of me. It was only one of the thousands of other ravines that isolated and cut off the rocks of the desert, and which also ran eastward. Within the ravine itself stretched a low range of hills, a miniature version of the great plateau of the Hebron mountains; this also ran into the deep depression of the Dead Sea.

In the center of the valley lay Bethlehem. Its houses spread
over two hills that lifted themselves above the floor of the valley.
My gaze swept over the streets of the town in the hope of finding
some clue about what had happened near it a few days before.
But I found no trace of this. Peace had stamped its impress on
the place. The trees in the courtyards adorned the impressive
stone houses with wreaths of green. This earthy scene also had a
certain heavenly touch, in the shape of round-domed churches
whose high spires rose far above the roofs of the houses. The
crosses climbed even higher than the tops of the spires, as if they
wanted to force their way through to the piece of sky that joined
the peaks of the Hebron mountains and the Judean hills.

"Why are you staring over there?" He sounded curious.

"Are you in a hurry?"

"Yes, I have to be in the outpost next to the Bethlehem road."

"You know what?" I suggested. "Go along there, and I'll join
you in about ten minutes. I want to get the feel of the terrain."

"Alright," Ilan agreed. "But watch those damn snipers."

"Be seeing you."

He gave me a friendly wave. I could make out the thick,
stubby fingers of his hand as it waved. "See you."

He went off, and I sat down on a rock next to one of the pine
trees scattered around the area. I went on scanning the graduated
slopes that surrounded the twin hills of Bethlehem like rings. On
the shiny black asphalt road winding between the houses of the
town, I could make out the movement of men and vehicles.

The boom of a shot broke in my ears. I threw myself to the
ground. The sound of an explosion reverberated in the valleys
around, like a chain of staccato thunder. From the pine tree that
stood in front of me, a hail of pine needles fell down, and I heard
the wings of a frightened raven who fled from its hideout with

scared cawing. Absolute quiet. I peered through the stems of the thorn bushes that covered the earth. From the houses on the slope came sounds of commotion and muffled shots. An impulse drove me to crawl to the place. I made good progress, until I came to a row of foxholes dug next to the barbed-wire fence that stretched along the Bethlehem road.

"What happened?" I puffed in the face of a soldier who peered out of the foxhole.

"A sniper got Ilan."

"Is it serious?"

"Wounded in the leg. They're taking him to the first-aid post." He gestured to the nearby building. I hurried there. Ilan was lying on a stretcher, with a few soldiers gathered around him. A gray woolen blanket covered his body. His pale face turned to me. I could see clearly the expression of shock in his eyes. They looked much bigger.

"You can have the field glasses," he groaned, looking at them. They were lying on the ground. "You wanted them."

"Yes, don't worry about it." I was embarrassed. "How do you feel?"

"It'll be OK," he tried to reassure me. "Got me in the leg." Sweat covered his face, and his swollen lips quivered with weakness.

The soldiers took hold of the stretcher, picked it up carefully, and went out to the company headquarters. Ilan's head shook about and lolled, turning toward me. There was a hint of apology in his glance, as if he was asking my pardon for the interruption of the reconnaissance trip. I waved goodbye to him. He smiled sadly until he disappeared from my sight.

I made my way back to the company headquarters slowly, getting there about ten minutes later. The secretary stood in the courtyard. "What's happened to Ilan?" I asked her.

"He's gone to the hospital in Jerusalem."

"Is he badly hurt?"

"The doctor has sent him to the hospital."

"Well, if he says so." I didn't think a wound in the leg needed treatment in a hospital.

Ilan died suddenly the next day. The doctors stated that this was caused by a blood clot. But I knew for sure, just knew, that he died because that had been his fate. No other reason. When I first heard the news, I couldn't grasp it, and didn't move a muscle—until the awareness of the tragedy sank in.

It was strange that after I had reconciled myself to his death, the image of his features became blurred in my memory. But I still held the field glasses he had left behind for me. When I gripped them tightly, thoughts flashed through my mind, rushed up and down my brain . . . *Ilan* . . . *He used to live near the seashore. That's what he had told me. I also used to live there, in a faded yellow house, whose paint was peeling from the walls because of the winds from the sea.* I tried hard to remember if I had met him as a boy. He may have been one of the kids in the nearby suburb. In my memory arose a winter day: a stormy, windswept sea, whipping foam on the waves, and a thin mist, cold and whitish, hovering on the face of the waters and spreading on the shore.

Children stood on the sand, collecting wooden planks and broken barrels thrown from the ships that crashed on the rocks off Jaffa. From time to time the waves thrust forward, and the children fled with happy cries. Then the waves retreated, leaving on the coast traces of oil and tar, which floated on the surface of the waters. The children began fighting among themselves over a piece of broad, dark wood, which had been thrown up on the shore. In my mind's eye I could see their faces, heated by the argument. I stood some distance away from them, but I didn't intervene. I listened to the sound of the sea. The incessant noise of the waves sounded harsh and rough at first. But slowly I became used to them, and they sounded like a faint humming, soft and prolonged, rather like a seashell put close to one's ear. The children were still quarreling over the wooden beam. A black, oily plank. Now I remembered what it had looked like, and it occurred to me that it was nothing but a floating coffin. A black coffin. Ilan was dead.

On the same day, I went out to the field again—the field that looked out at Bethlehem.

"I'm going out to look for enemy snipers," I informed the company commander. But in my heart there was already a dull feeling that every human target across the border would be fair game for me. A wild impulse forced me to hunt down human prey.

With elastic steps, like a hunter walking on tiptoe, I reached the rock on which I'd sat the day before. I lay flat on the ground. The valley lay spread out before me like an empty watermelon shell. My pricked-up ears caught the rustle of the thorn stems and the treetops moving in the quiet wind. My searching eyes didn't discover any target in the area. *Never mind,* I thought to myself, *I still have plenty of time.*

Once more I looked over the part of the front I could see. The long wait made me notice something I hadn't realized before: the movement and life latent in every clod of earth. The beginning of this revelation was limited to the area lying literally under my nose. The thin, long stalks of wild grass drew my attention to their minute motion. Looking at them casually, I noticed that no two stalks moved in the same way. For a moment it seemed that they were breathing and alive as if they were made to move by a pulse of life. After looking still harder, I noticed a marked difference between each of the stalks, and in the texture of the fibers, which gave a distinctive fingerprint to every stalk.

I went on to examine the thorn bushes that were scattered all over the area. Their dry branches waved in the air with a staccato, nervous shudder. Here too I found a hidden independence in every prickly arm that moved in its own special, private rhythm. The constant movement of the weeds and thorn bushes united to form a glittering sea of shuddering and incessant movement. Inside it, in the dense, tangled undergrowth of grass and bushes, ladybugs crawled about. I held a hand out to the nearest ladybug, but I didn't touch it, for fear of crushing it. Since boyhood I had been taught not to harm this tiny, delicate insect, with its shiny red cover and black dots. This was really ironic. My heart was full of compassion for this ordinary little insect, while my gun was ready to take another human being's life.

I looked further off, to the trees. Their branches moved. Now I could make out the movement of each branch of the trees, the quivering motion of the leaves, like fish caught in a net. Here was a tiny, almost invisible motion of the slow-moving trunks, and here too I discovered the restrained independence in every leaf, like the leaf that fell off not far from me and continued blowing about.

Captivated by the perpetual motion of the greenery, I peered once more at the open spaces of the valley. Through the round window of the field glasses, everything seemed to be moving. The crosses on the spires of the churches looked as if they were hovering in the air, like birds spreading out. Suddenly the blood rushed to my head. There was a man in front of me! Not more than five hundred meters away. He marched along the whitish stone fence that stretched like a thick rope up the slope of the mountain. He was making for the fields behind the ridge, and would have to pass over the open stony plateau that met the end of the fence. Here the road began to wind and twist, and he would have to slow down. That would be a good moment to hit him, against the clear background of the white stones.

Eagerly, keenly, like a hunting dog that sticks close to its prey, I followed the slow walk of my quarry. With a cold calculation I estimated the height of the target, in order to aim my gun straight at its center. The blade of the rear gun sight rested on the imaginary center of the man I wanted to kill.

The wooden butt, which pressed so hard against the flesh of my right cheek, caught my eye. A faint spark of light was thrown from the back of the polished wood. A long line of broken light danced on the luminous brown butt. The fragile ray of sun bothered me. I passed my thumb impatiently along the wood where the light struck it, in order to cover up and hide the reflection that shone right into my eyes.

I was eager to press the trigger, and this soon became a burning desire. The pressure of my clenched hand on the trigger made me feel a sharp twinge of pain in the tensed muscles of my whole hand. At the same time, I sensed a sort of dull pleasure, the kind one feels in waiting for something exciting and anticipated. I was caught up in a new desire, one I had never known before. It swept me off my feet. I couldn't oppose it. The nearer my target came to the sights, the weaker my resistance became. My mind was drained of all thought, and the whole of my being was focused on the finger held against the trigger. Now I felt the slight tremor of my finger even more than before. The finger carried my body with it, like a tiny but powerful crane, and dragged it forward to the black edge of the rifle. The front rifle sight was now touching the target, who slowed down, turned around a little, and then stopped. The blade of the sight blended

into the figure. Now the man was trapped in the dead center of
the sight. My breath stopped. My finger closed on the trigger
with a slow, springy motion.

The gun thundered, recoiled, and sank at once into the
hollow of my shoulder. The end of the barrel moved in front
of me, hiding the target from my sight. I pushed the gun down
excitedly and stared at the rocky terrain, which stuck out as white
as the sails of a lonely ship in the wide expanse of a murky sea.

Where was he? I lifted the field glasses and swept them hurriedly over every rock and clod of earth. Had I hit him? I thought
I had. But I couldn't be sure. I went on searching for some sign or
other. Even if I hadn't actually hit him, it was obvious that I had
frightened him, or so I consoled myself, anyway. This made me
very happy. It wasn't a feeling of hatred, or even one of personal
animosity. At that moment the concept of "enemy" had lost its
meaning. Suddenly the idea of shooting at another man gave me
a feeling of intoxication.

From that day onward I began to enjoy sniping. Every now
and then I went out to look for targets. I lay in wait for the enemy
snipers who fired at us from the stone building in the center of
the stony hill. I also became used to shooting at animals, and in
the course of time this became a daily habit.

The next day some new soldiers arrived, the section I was
going to take over. They looked like a wild bunch. They were
standing in the courtyard of the company headquarters when
I saw them first. They weren't standing in a proper line, and
their guns were swung carelessly over their shoulders. They
glanced around with expressions that showed their contempt
and dissatisfaction. The fact that they had to wait for me didn't
seem to please them.

"I'm the deputy section commander," said the full-faced,

swarthy fellow who stood in front of the row. "My name is Sasson," he introduced himself with a smile. He paused for a moment and then went on: "There're fifteen of us here. Counting me, of course."

"Been here long?"

"More than two weeks." He smiled happily, exposing a row of gleaming white teeth. He went on, still smiling: "Before that I was an assistant to the instructor in the training camp." When he finished, he continued looking at me. The constant grinning annoyed and provoked me. It contained something I didn't care for, something which made me very angry at that particular moment. Maybe it was the self-confidence that shone out of his vigorous face, or the expression of strength in his prominent cheekbones, or his stubborn, square-cut chin. What did I have against him? Was I annoyed because he showed the self-confidence I lacked myself? He looked straight at me, as if waiting for an answer, and this broke the chain of my thought.

"Yes," I answered, "you can help me a lot." Some grumbling sounds came from the other soldiers, and I heard a loud whistle. "Any complaints?" I asked in a soft voice. The soldiers were watching every movement of my face. A rustle of excitement and amusement came from the ranks. "You!" I shouted suddenly, wildly at the first soldier I happened to see. "Do you have any complaints?" I repeated the question again, provocatively, fixing my eyes on his. He tried to move his gaze, but couldn't.

"No, no," he stammered. Quiet, complete quiet. I could see the surprised look in his fellow soldiers' eyes. The silence seemed like a good moment to walk along the straggling line and take a closer look at them. My eyes met a familiar face. Detected a hint of a sneer. But a second look told me this was

only embarrassment. It was Benny. I remembered him from
the depot for greenhorns.

"Don't I know you from somewhere?"

"Yes," he answered. "From the depot." His dark eyes rested
on me quietly.

"I'll talk to you later." I then turned toward the other soldiers. "And now," I said, "we'll go off to the outpost. Follow me,
in single file. And watch out for snipers." They looked scared at
the prospect of being hit.

"They're firing from the hill opposite," I couldn't help adding, with sadistic pleasure.

"I've got a stomachache." One man stepped out of the line.
"Where can I have a shit?"

"Go to the forest," I said angrily. "And hurry up."

He rushed off, while the other men encouraged him.

"He's a real character, that guy," one of them chortled.

"Oh, that Shabtai," Sasson snorted in disdain. "He's shitting
in his pants already. What'll happen when things really get hot?"

"Then he'll get chronic diarrhea," someone said, and everyone laughed.

These jokes at Shabtai's expense went on until he came
back. He went to his place in the line, still tightening the belt
of his pants.

"Well, I hope you're feeling better now," Sasson jeered at him
loftily.

"And now," I shouted, trying to sound very serious, "follow
me—in one row."

I marched forward, and the soldiers followed me in a
single line.

CHAPTER 7

NIGHT

That same night the company commander came along to inspect us. He made a lightning tour of the positions, and then sat down to talk to me behind the protective wall. "Everything alright?" he asked loudly.

"Well, more or less," I hemmed and hawed. "The boys look a bit green . . ."

"What's that?" he shouted, as if he couldn't believe his ears.

"Yes, greenhorns," I screamed back. "Green as little apples!"

"So make them work for their living!" he yelled back. "Rub the skin off their arses!"

"Easy to say so!"

"Why don't you take some of them out on a patrol tonight," he interrupted me, as if he hadn't heard what I'd just said. A thought crossed my mind: maybe it suited him to pretend to be deaf sometimes. "Go down to the valley," he added. "Always plenty of scouts moving around there. In the white house at the end of the village, there's a regional headquarters. I want you to get hold of some scouts and documents. I need information." He paused for a moment. "And don't do anything stupid," he added. "We've lost enough men lately."

"Alright," I blurted unwillingly.

"That will give you a chance to let the boys really have a work-out," the commander added, as if trying to spur me on. He laughed faintly, looking around. When he saw I had nothing to add, he went off, remarking as he left: "If you have any problems, let me know."

After he'd gone, I called Sasson. "We'll go out on a patrol tonight. We'll go out in a four-man team. You, me, and two others. Who would you suggest? You know them better than I do."

Sasson thought for a moment. "They've never been in action before."

"I know, but all the same . . ." I pressed him.

"Let's take Shimon. He's a steady fellow, rather nervous, but he'll be OK."

"And perhaps Benny. I know him from the training camp."

"He doesn't feel well today," Sasson dismissed him. "Said he'd caught a cold."

"Oh!" I exclaimed, as if I understood. "Well, then, who else is there?"

"What about Shabtai? Sure, he looked a bit soft today. But that boy has guts." I nodded in agreement.

"We'll set off in an hour," I proposed. "We'll meet next to the armory."

At the appointed time, all of us gathered there.

"Will we be out for long?" Shimon asked in a faint voice.

"As long as necessary," Sasson reprimanded him. Shimon hung his head, as if in shame. It was obvious that he wanted to ask something else, but he didn't.

"I've already told them what they have to do." Sasson seemed to expect me to praise him for being so prompt. I was silent for a moment, ignoring him, and I could sense him putting on a sour expression. His anger pleased me.

"Right, we're going," I whispered. "And keep absolutely quiet." We began moving down the slope that wound down into the valley. A dark, starless sky pressed above us, like a sort of purple curtain over the valley, with its edges hanging at the ends of the shadowy ridges that closed in around us. The marchers' feet thudded with a sound that disturbed the fragile quiet. From time to time the dogs of the village barked, and this piercing sound built up into a nervous chorus. Then the barking died down completely, and once more the only noise was the clatter of our feet over the stones.

The more we walked and the deeper we went into the valley, the closer its sides seemed to press, until its bottom appeared like the gaping mouth of a prehistoric beast. We halted next to a low stone fence at the bottom of the valley, whose shadow fell on the limestone like a threatening, ominous black line that could not be crossed. The dark shadow of the trees crystallized, shrank, and changed into a heavy black stain that rose above the surrounding sea of darkness like a dangerous reef. Only the smooth white stones went on winking at us clearly.

A growing feeling of danger came over me. In the shadow of the fence, I bent down to the ground, motioning to the soldiers to do the same.

Lying on the damp ground, I gave myself over entirely to listening to the sounds of the night. Frogs croaked. Where did they spring from? Were we near a stream or a swamp? The croaking grew louder and became more discordant . . . Even as a boy I had disliked frogs. They revolted me . . . My ears pricked up suddenly, and my senses became sharper. I heard another sound, a muffled rustling and scraping in the valley.

Sasson turned his head toward me, with an expression that showed that he realized what was going on. Then, we lifted ourselves above the fence and pointed our guns slowly toward the unknown people who were coming toward us. We couldn't see them yet. In front of us loomed the long shadows of tree trunks. For a moment it seemed like the trunks had swollen and grown thicker, until they took on the dimensions of legendary giants. Tense quiet prevailed. The sound of steps faded away for a moment and then returned. Through the shadowy trunks, the feet of the marching men appeared, and then, suddenly, they came into full view. There were two of them. Their clothes attracted my attention. Narrow trousers with cuffs made even narrower by clips. On their heads were keffiyeh, the ends tucked into the necks of their battledress. These were the enemies. They marched straight toward the muzzle of my submachine gun. Their hands swung back and forth, as if they were out for a refreshing evening stroll. My eyes were caught by one of their glistening hands closed on the shadowy submachine gun that hung downward loosely and with a feeling of casual restfulness. The sight of the gun gave me a shock. For a second I found myself stepping backward, as if an invisible foot had struck me in the face. But I stopped myself. The shapes came closer. My stomach went hard. My breathing sounded too loud, too pronounced. My nostrils whistled. I opened my mouth wide and breathed through it in order to quiet my breathing.

When they were about twenty strides away from the fence, they slowed down. They stopped and stood still, lowering their heads as if looking for something. While doing so, they turned around. One of them put out his hand to catch the end of his keffiyeh, which was flapping in the wind. He took hold of it with a vigorous movement and tucked it back in to his battle dress.

"Go ahead," he ordered his companion in a thin, strident voice.

His mate murmured in agreement and they resumed their walking. At that moment the quiet was suddenly broken. A clatter of stones and the sound of a strangled cough. Their peaceful stance became tense at once. They sprinted madly toward the lower land on their right, as if they sensed what was about to happen.

I fired, and Sasson and the others did so at the same time. The bent shape of a man flew up against the violet sky. His hands moved feverishly, like the hands of a drowning man struggling with the waves. Suddenly his hands were thrown behind him and his body, whose movement had been cut off, strayed from its path, twisted, and gave a strangled cry: "Ahhhh." Then the figure fell to the ground and vanished from my sight.

"The other one ran away." Sasson's excited voice filtered to me through the sound of the shots. "Who was the idiot that made such a noise?" Sasson shouted when the shooting stopped. The two soldiers raised their heads above the fence, and Sasson came forward on the other side of the trees.

"What? The second one escaped?" Shimon exclaimed in a surprised voice.

"Wait here," I ordered them. "We'll see what's happened with the one we hit."

I crawled to the black spot on the ground that indicated where the body was lying. His feet were sprawled wide. For some reason his boots looked bigger than usual. The way he was lying made me certain he was dead. I came close enough to him to be within arm's reach of the body. It gave off a sourish smell of sweat. I put my hand out toward his leg and lifted it a little. Its weight astonished me. I let it fall to the ground, and it made a muffled sound. I forced myself to examine his face from close up. Two glassy, wide-open eyes.

Sasson returned in a crouched run. "He's fled," he confirmed, in a disappointed tone. The short silence was broken by a volley of machine gun shots from the enemy positions in the nearby village. A blinding rocket went off with a flash. Its white light froze my movements. It floated heavenward and then began floating with irritating slowness to the light-stricken center of the valley.

The rocket went out, and the darkness came back. Twice as dark as before. "Can you see what you've done, you donkey?" I heard the frightened voice of Shabtai reprimanding his mate. "Couldn't you hold your cough back?"

"Smart guy," the other soldier jeered back. "You're quite a hero, eh? Only yesterday you shit in your pants when you heard about the snipers . . ."

"Who, me?" Shabtai tried to respond, but Sasson stopped the two of them.

"Which of you coughed?" he asked in a grave voice.

"We must get out of here right away, before they bring more men along," I interrupted.

"Well, what shall we do with the body?" Sasson insisted.

"We'll have to search his clothes. Maybe he had some documents or papers."

"Well, let's have a look."

"No, not here. We must get out of here. I don't want to get stuck in the area with two greenhorns like these. They've already given us enough trouble. We'll take the body with us. Once we're back in camp, we can search it properly."

"Must we take the body with us?" Sasson asked.

"What's the fuss about? We're only five hundred meters from the camp. Let's drag him there and get out of here before they spot us."

Sasson signaled to the other two, who came a little closer. "Come here and lift him up," he ordered.

"What for?" one of them called out in a choked voice. "He's dead."

"Pick him up and come," I repeated Sasson's order. "We have to search his clothes. And we can't do it here. We've got to get out of here as soon as we can!"

"As you like," they grumbled, bending down and lifting the body. "He's bloody heavy."

"Come on," I whispered, bending down and picking up the enemy soldier's abandoned machine gun. The two of them began marching heavily, carrying the body. I glanced at the ground to see that nothing had been left behind, and then made a hurried inspection of the machine gun. It scared me. It looked as if it would go off by itself. I took the bullets out and hung the gun over my shoulder. I gave another hurried look around me and joined the others with rapid strides. We labored up the slope to the base camp. The distance of five hundred meters passed with maddening slowness. Every few steps, the two soldiers carrying the body stumbled and fell, and then the body fell to the ground with a heavy thud.

"Let's take over," I suggested to Sasson when I heard the soldiers' labored breathing as they bent over the body, trying to lift him again. "They sound like a couple of steam engines," I added contemptuously. Sasson came up to the body and pushed the two away.

"OK, let's get this over with."

He bent over the dead man's head and lifted the upper part of his body to a sitting position. I also bent down and took hold of the legs, which lay sprawled open carelessly, placing them together and pulling them upward toward me. A smell of dirty feet rose in my nostrils. The body was lifted off the ground. We began marching quickly, and this made our burden sway from side to side. Now I realized why the two other men had become so tired. The body was subject to a force of gravity that dragged it toward the ground. It fell out of my hands and slid downward slowly while I struggled with all my might to bring it back to a horizontal position again. This strange fight and the march up the steep slope flooded my face with trickles of sweat, a cold sweat that burned like frost. My feet also became ten times as heavy because of the mud that clung to the soles of my boots.

The nausea and stomach cramps that had bothered me of late came back to trouble me. But this time I felt even worse. The corpse I was carrying made me feel sick. I was at the point of vomiting. But I stopped myself, because I didn't want to lose face in front of the men I was supposed to command. The shadow of the barbed-wire fence around our outpost showed itself faintly. A voice called out: "Who's there?" The sentry had seen us. I breathed more easily.

"It's us," Sasson answered.

"What's the password?" The sentry was standing firm.

"Bar Giora," Sasson snapped out. But he added angrily: "Why the hell are you acting like such an idiot? After all, you identified us!"

The sentry didn't answer. We came up to the edge of the fence and threw the body on the ground, with a feeling of relief.

"Who's that?" The sentry was taken aback by the corpse. When no one responded, he said, as if to himself: "Yes, I heard the shots . . ."

"Let's take him to the armory," Sasson suggested. We began dragging the body through the barbed-wire fence. "Now you two can take him along," he ordered Shimon and Shabtai.

They lifted the body reluctantly and marched off toward the dark building. Sasson, who hurried in front of them, opened the door of the armory. The body was taken inside and placed on the ground.

The light bulb threw a circle of clear light, which seemed to encircle the corpse while leaving the rest of the room in darkness. Two bloodstains spread over the tightly-bound robes. They marked the places where the bullets had hit him, in the chest and the stomach. The dead man's head lay to one side, stretched back, as if he were watching something now hidden from sight. His face was turned toward the ceiling, his staring eyes wide open and fixed. This position made his head face the focal point of light from the yellow bulb hanging above him. The centralized lighting gave his dark skin a sickly glow. Two deep shadows lay in the sunken hollows of his cheeks. I was amazed by the change that had taken place in the size of his body and limbs. His skull had also shrunken. At the same time, his shoes seemed to have gotten bigger. Sasson and I bent over the body and began searching the pockets of the bloodstained robe.

"Nothing," Sasson ejaculated, pulling out a packet of cigarettes wet with blood.

"Mmmm," I murmured, revolted by the sight of the blood that stuck to my fingers. I stretched out my hand to the trousers of the dead man and began wiping my fingers on them. "Let's look in his shirt," I went on, after I'd finished this. We opened the buttons of his robe and rolled his sweater, until we came across the pockets of a khaki shirt. But here too there was nothing of any military value. Now it was the turn of the trouser pockets: money, a bunch of keys, a comb.

"Bugger all," Sasson exclaimed in disappointment, straightening his back. He wrinkled his forehead in thought and then added: "Maybe there's something hidden on his body?" He looked at me inquiringly. "Well, shall we start?" he asked. I nodded.

We began running our hands along the length and breadth of the body, turning it over when we had done one side. While we were still busy, I glanced toward the two white-faced soldiers standing in the doorway. Shimon, who didn't notice me looking at him, turned toward his comrade and whispered something to him that brought me to my feet: "Butcher."

"Who's a butcher?" I yelled, turning toward him with a threatening expression.

"I didn't mean it . . ." Shimon stammered. "I really didn't mean it."

"I suppose you think that I enjoy poking around a dead man's pockets," I hissed through my clenched teeth, bringing my face close to his. A light film of moisture, a network of tiny sweat beads covered his forehead and lips. He stepped back until he stood against the wall of the room.

"Well," I snapped, "now you can go to him and finish the search."

"I can't . . . I can't." He began sobbing quietly.

"And I suppose it's easy for me, eh?"

"Look at his skin," Shimon wept. "I can't touch it. This lamp is driving me crazy." Shimon stopped for a moment, passing his palm over his damp forehead. "I don't feel well," he wailed in a choked voice.

"Neither do I."

"Leave him alone. Can't you see his nerves are gone?" I heard Sasson's soothing voice. "Look," he added, gazing at the body, "his pants are wet with piss." The words calmed my anger. I gave Shimon an accusing look and returned to Sasson.

"Does he have an identity disc?" I asked.

"As if you have one!"

"You're right, come to think of it. I haven't got one either. Actually, we aren't soldiers, but bloody civilians."

"Bloody is right," Shabtai chimed in.

"At last Shabtai's said something!" Sasson made fun of him.

"So we don't seem to have found anything?" I summed up in a disappointed tone.

"No," Sasson confirmed sadly.

"Well, then we have to bury him."

"He has a wristwatch. Shall we bury it with him?"

I bent over the dead man's hand, which lay stretched out on the floor. A shining silver watch was fastened to his wrist with a black leather strap. The curly hairs on the pale, lifeless skin stood up straight all around the curved edges of the watch, their ends coated by dead man's sweat. I could sense the smell of the graveyard on them. I took a step backward.

"A Swiss Omega watch," Sasson announced. "Do you want it?"

"No," I answered, feeling my flesh creep. "We'll bury him with it. This is the only identity mark he has. It's a sort of disc that will remain after his body rots away. Perhaps one day they will be able to identify him by the watch. He may have relations. Or something like that . . ."

"And who hasn't?" Shabtai observed in a soft voice.

"Yes," Sasson sighed, "he was young."

"We're all young," Shabtai added gloomily. Sasson gave him a sharp look, as if he wanted to say: "Well, would you like the old people to go out and fight?" Silence.

"Take some spades and dig a grave," I broke the silence, looking at Shabtai and Shimon.

"Where?" they asked.

"Find some soft soil. Perhaps in the copse . . ."

"Yes, that's a good place," Sasson agreed. "And make it quick. We must finish this business once and for all." The two of them left the room with slow steps. I went out after them to the front stoop of the armory. From there I watched their painfully slow movements. They dragged their feet over the rocky ground, making rustling noises. My ears picked up the sound of the wind, whistling between the branches of the trees with a wailing sound, like the choked groans of frightened children. Then the wind stopped, and I could hear the soldiers' footsteps again. A short silence followed, broken only by the sound of distant shots. These were joined by the strong but muffled sound of the spades striking against the rocky soil. For a long time I stood on the porch, silent and staring into the night. Sasson stood next to me. He didn't want to stay in the room with the dead man.

"We're finished," came Shabtai's rasping voice. We turned toward him. He and Shimon stood a few yards away. Strange, I thought to myself, that I did not notice them when they came close to me.

"Did you dig deep enough?" Sasson asked.

"It'll go in!" Shimon answered angrily.

"Well, then take him out," Sasson said out of the side of his mouth. Without saying a word, we all strode toward the armory. We went in and stopped next to the body.

"Two take his hands and two his feet," I suggested. I put my foot on the submachine gun, which lay on the ground, and moved it into the corner of the room.

"What about this?" Shabtai asked, looking at the submachine gun.

"We need it."

"It's not like in the films," Sasson chimed in. "Here we don't stick the dead soldier's gun into the mound over his grave."

"No," I blurted out, "but we'll put in one of the wooden poles from the barbed-wire fence. That will take the place of the gun." I regarded giving a pole like this, which we were short of ourselves, for the enemy's grave as a sacrifice on our part.

"We're tired," Shimon said. "Why don't you call some other guys to help you finish the job? It's not easy."

"The others are asleep already. Thank God you're burying someone and not being buried yourselves. That could also have happened to you," Sasson rebuked him. "Don't think I've forgotten the noise you kicked up during the ambush, or that I've forgiven you. These things can cost lives."

"What a life!" Shabtai sighed, with a trace of irony, but also as if he accepted the verdict. Without wasting any more words, the four of us bent down and took the dead man by his hands and feet. His back sank down until it almost touched the ground. As we walked, he bumped against the ground from time to time. Finally, Sasson said: "That's it."

We stood at the edge of the pit that had just been dug. We let the body lie at the brink of the grave. One of its arms hung inside, moving about slightly.

"Yes, that's it," I repeated. I bent down and began pushing the corpse into the grave. It slipped down and fell onto the bottom of the hole, with a frozen thud.

"Cover it up!" Sasson ordered the two soldiers who stood there like fossils. They took their spades from the mound of piled earth which had been heaped up on the side, and began shoveling the earth into the grave.

"When you've finished, you can go back to your huts. I'm going to the armory," I told the three men. Without waiting for their reply, I went off. The sentry who stalked up and down in front of the armory looked at me expectantly, as if waiting

for me to tell him what had happened. But I ignored his un-
spoken request and went back to my room. My gaze fell on
the submachine gun that had been flung to the ground. I bent
over it and picked it up. It was a British Sten-5 type. Its reddish
butt attracted my fingers, which began tapping and patting the
polished wooden edges.

Fatigue, thoughts rising and sinking. A pinching pressure in
my chest. A blank feeling spread through my head. Its center lay
on the inner edges of my temples. I felt as if I had sunk myself in
filth, in muck. The congealed blood that had dried on my hands
and on my shirt made me feel dirty. My skin had become stubborn and heavy, as if it didn't belong to me, as if it was a foreign
organ whose touch was revolting. If I could have stripped it off
me, I would have done so willingly . . . A painful desire to wash
myself seized me. To wash . . . to bathe . . . to purify myself . . .

I lifted the submachine gun quickly and ran toward my room.
I took a towel from the bed and ran back to the tap outside the
room. Despite the biting cold, I stripped off all my clothes, turned
on the tap, and plunged into its ice-cold stream. My breath
stopped. My whole body curled up like a hedgehog, as if fleeing
from the frosty teeth that bit into my flesh. I continued standing
under the tap, rubbing myself, rubbing and shrinking into my
skin with the vestiges of my flagging strength. But the frost won.
I shut the tap and threw the towel over myself, rubbing myself
briskly until waves of warmth flooded my body. The feeling of
pollution weakened but didn't go away entirely. I put my clothes
on and went back to the room.

There I threw myself on the cool cloth of the camp bed. But
even there my thoughts wouldn't leave me alone. I turned over
on my back, fixing my eyes on the ceiling. An empty darkness.
Eldad's greenish eyes emerged from the black. Their stabbing

look sent a cold shudder over my skin. Eyes without a body. Two
lonely eyes hanging in the vacuum that surrounded me. The
eyes began to retreat. They grew smaller until they disappeared
completely and merged into the hollowness. The sound of wild
laughter. Its roaring echo rolled and grew louder, rang in my ears.
Two spots of white shone in the darkness and swept toward me.
They took on giant dimensions, a double row of yellow, rotting
teeth leaning forward crookedly. The teeth grew closer, until
I could make out a blurred face. The enemy. Swarthy skin. A
mouth twisted in an expression of hatred. Burning eyes. His lips
were covered by spit and a disgusting moisture. The laughter gave
way to a murderous shriek: "Kill! Kill!" Now the full shape of the
enemy appeared in all its clarity. He grasped a long knife in his
hand and pointed it at me. I raised myself up from my place in
despair, aiming a submachine gun at him. There was a foul taste
in my mouth. A pungent taste of vomit rose from my belly and
lodged between the crevices of my teeth and on the tiny pores of
my tongue. I stared around me. The walls closed in on all sides,
making me terrified, hampering my breathing, giving me a feeling of loss, like the feeling of a lonely man drowning and about
to be swallowed up by a giant wave, which would sweep him away.
My eyes dashed about in panic from one side to another, looking
for some ray of light and hope. Here was a spot of light from the
window. With a leap I jumped toward it, pressing my burning face
against the cold glass. Through the iron bars in the opening, I
could see violet skies. My breathing calmed down and grew easier.

With hesitant steps I returned to the bed. Once more I
lay there with my eyes wide open. But I couldn't escape my
thoughts. This time I was worried about the war. The last news
had been depressing. *Will we win? After all, the enemy outnumbers
us dozens of times.* A storm of panic took hold of me suddenly.

I must get out of here! Out of this town—anywhere! To escape, to flee!,
an inner voice beat wildly against my brain. Another voice, more
relaxed and soothing, slapped me in my heated face: *It's impossible
to run away . . . You can't do it . . . You can't escape!*

My head sank down onto the bed again. My hand clutched
my chest. Something was stirring inside me. My heart was contracting, becoming harder and harder, turning to stone, as if it
had shrunk and was becoming lost in the hollow of my chest. A
flaming dizziness turned inside my head, trickled down behind
my forehead, and relaxed the tautness of my skin. Then I felt the
tears that stood in my eyes. But my crying was choked before it
managed to break out, and my tears stopped in the corners of
my eyes. I couldn't let them flow out. And then I realized that I
had lost the ability to cry. It was gone, vanished almost overnight.
I shut my eyes in despair and buried my face in the cool cloth
strips of the rough bed.

CHAPTER 8

THE STAINS

The next morning I took a rifle from the armory and went off to the forest, looking for the mound that marked the grave between the trees. My heart toyed with the vain hope that the events of the previous night had been nothing but a deception. But I didn't really believe this myself. The wooden pole stuck in the ground rose up like the upright of a gallows. I swallowed my spit and walked forward as bravely as I could. The pole leaned to one side. The two soldiers had done a hurried job. The end of the pole was wet with morning dew. For a moment my eyes strayed stealthily to the mound itself. The dampness of the fresh, porous soil sent a cold shudder through my spine. I couldn't take my eyes off the pole.

I began walking away, sad and depressed. Was it sorrow for the enemy soldier who had died—or for myself? A shot fired close by severed the thread of my thoughts. I turned my head toward the snipers' hills and sprinted toward the positions on the slope, instinctively. Weak shouts: "Orderly! Orderly! I've been hit!" I rushed madly toward the place where I thought the wounded man might be, bumping into a group of soldiers bending over him. Where had they sprung from? I was pleased by their promptness.

"It's Shmuel," one of them remarked. The wounded man's hand was stained with bright blood.

"Take him to the first-aid station," I called out in an excited voice, gazing at his closed eyes.

"Don't tell my folks about it," he groaned. "Don't let them know." He opened his eyes for a moment, giving us a pleading look.

"Don't worry, we won't tell them."

The soldiers dragged him up the slope, moaning with pain. I crawled to the foxhole in front of the fence, and from there I peered out at the hill in front of us. I couldn't see any movement around the building. I concentrated on finding a way to eliminate the snipers. The sound of stones sliding down the slopes made me turn around. Sasson jumped inside, breathing heavily.

"They've taken him to the first-aid station," he panted. In that moment an idea flashed into my mind.

"I've got it!" I cried out happily, slapping him on the shoulder.

"Got what?"

"I think I know how to polish off these bastards." I stopped, trying to work out the plan in my mind. A glint of light from the stone on the hill caught my eye. Silver strips, glistening, breaking up into thousands of fragile slivers of lightning. Almost like sweat pouring from the naked forehead of the rocks. The shining drops of morning dew trickled over the rocky slopes.

"Well, what's the plan?" he asked again.

"We'll give our sniper pals a little surprise tonight. Have you noticed that they only operate in the daytime?"

"Yes, that's right."

"Well, tonight we'll go to their place and stick a few mines up their backsides. When they go back there tomorrow, they'll be finished. What d'you think?"

"Terrific. Why didn't I think of it?"

"We'll need three men. You, me, and we'll take someone else," I added, seeing in my mind's eye the thin wires of steel that we would stretch in front of the ruined building.

"Prepare hand grenades and steel wires. We'll set booby traps of half-open grenades. Get an electric pocket lamp also. We'll really let them have it this time." I hummed to myself happily, rubbing my belly with excitement.

Sasson left the forest, on his way to the armory. I went back, but this time I kept far away from the mound that covered the grave. I stopped in the shade of one of the pines and stretched myself out on the ground, under the tree. Through the branches, glistening islands of blue heaven floated backward and forward in the dark green sea. I felt a slight dizziness turning my head, and I shut my eyes. Through my closed lids filtered a dark patch pitted with heavy red spots. A drowsy fatigue seized me: a sort of daydream. The red stains crystallized and took on the shape of a dead body, with purple skin. Black cracks made clefts in the twisted, distorted body. I was not repelled in any way by what I saw. Joy filled my heart; a sweet, weary pleasure crept over me.

I began constructing in my mind the defeat of this body . . . A man covered by a khaki cloak and carrying a large rifle marched to the door of the ruined building. His heavy, hobnailed boots struck against the stones with a monotonous sound. The door was opened, and the boot, crossing the threshold, pulled the thin thread of steel. A flash. Large black eyes opened wide with horror and surprise. A pillar of flame filled the room. The four strong walls were shaken by a deafening explosion. The air blast hurled the rifle forcibly against the wall. I couldn't see what was happening because of the dense smoke. All I could see was a big, clumsy rifle smashed to smithereens, and splinters of wood from the butt scattered around the floor.

I jumped up from my place. Trunks of pine trees all around me. A smell of resin, coming from under the bark, gave me a pleasant shudder. What had happened? Was I dreaming, or had it really taken place? Were my eyes seeing things before they actually happened? Could I have discovered in myself a new sense, which had come to me because of the war? Hadn't I seen dark, ominous stains on Eldad's face the last time we met—the time he went off on a convoy from which he never returned? Yes, of course there had been spots on his face, and I was almost certain I had seen those faint spots on Ilan's face as well. I was positive I had noticed a stain on Yosef's face—Yosef who was killed at Sha'ar Hagai. Was I able to foresee people's death in battle? A cold feeling gripped me. The ground was damp, and I shuddered. I jumped up in a panic. I ached to get hold of a mirror and look in it. Maybe there were spots on my face as well? I ran toward my room, so eager to get to a mirror that I wasn't as careful as usual about the snipers. A bullet whistled not far from me. I fell to the ground, and went on crawling until I reached the door of my room.

My panting, puffing face, covered with dust, looked back at me in the mirror that shook in my hand. *Were there spots on my face?* I examined myself closely. *I don't see any spots . . . None at all? Are you sure?*

A dark cloud gathered in the corner of my forehead, stamping on it dark, almost invisible freckles hidden just beneath the skin. *No. It's impossible. I must be imagining things.* I put the mirror down on the bed and collapsed onto it, completely exhausted. I fell asleep.

A loud knock at the door. "Come in!" I shouted, annoyed at being woken up so suddenly. I saw Sasson's worried face.

Still caught up in sleep, I saw at first only his moving lips. "What are you talking about?" I asked, sitting up and rubbing my eyes with my fists.

"That guy Shimon. You remember, the one who gave us that trouble last night. Seems to have gone crazy."

"Who has?" I began waking up.

"Half an hour ago he grabbed a chopper from the storeroom and burst outside. He shouted that he's going to kill you. We tried to catch him, but he ran away to the wood."

"To kill me?" I exclaimed in amazement. Then I dismissed it with a laugh: "If he really wanted to kill me, he'd have taken a gun and not a chopper."

"That's the kind of thing you or I would do," Sasson insisted. "But not for him. He's crackers. He's nuts, I'm telling you."

"He's no crazier than anyone else," I replied angrily. "He's just a bluffer."

"No, he's not. You should have seen the way he foamed at the mouth . . ."

"Where is he now?"

"Hiding in the wood."

"OK, let's go and fetch him." I lifted myself up from my bed and took the submachine gun.

"Maybe we should take another few soldiers with us?" Sasson suggested diffidently.

"Not necessary. He only has a chopper, after all."

We went off toward the copse and began walking up the slope. The bare trunks of pine trees moved in front of us with giddy speed. I felt vomit rising from my belly. "Let's slow down a little," I suggested to Sasson. His steps slowed down. But a moment later we both stopped dead. A faint flicker of light flashed between the dense branches of the trees. Our gaze was drawn to the top of the hill. Shimon's shadow. He stood between the trees, the sun shining on his back. His face was in semi-darkness, so that his figure appeared like a black spot standing out against the background of the sky. He spotted us. But to our surprise he remained standing where he was, screaming at us as loudly as he could and waving the ax angrily above his head. We ran toward him. "I'll finish the two of you!" he yelled hoarsely, in a mighty voice. "I'll finish you off!"

We stopped about ten paces from him. He went on screaming madly, his mouth wide open, and only his lower jaw rising and falling as it uttered his oaths. His limbs contracted, compressed together, ready to dash forward. I lifted the submachine gun to my shoulder and aimed it straight at his eyes.

"Shimon," I said quietly, "put the ax on the ground. Otherwise you'll get a bullet right in your head."

He stopped shouting for a moment, giving me an astonished look.

"You," he panted furiously, "you!" His face puffed up with anger, and a nervous shudder passed through his fleshy cheeks. The hand holding the ax lifted with a menacing gesture.

"Throw the chopper on the ground!" I repeated my warning. "Or else you've had it. Hurry up. Throw it down!"

The hand that held the ax began to sink slowly, until it was completely down. But the ax was still not released.

"Shimon," I called, "listen to me. If you don't put that bloody chopper down right away, I'll pump you full of bullets. Get it?"

An astonished expression showed on his quivering face. His eyes grew damp, and the shudder grew and spread to his forehead.

"What do you want of my life?" he wept, in a hoarse voice. I started thinking that maybe he really was out of his mind.

"Put the chopper down and come here."

"And you won't do anything to me?" he asked in a naive tone.

"No, I won't do a thing." His eyes examined me, and I felt them drop until they confronted the muzzle of the gun aimed at him.

"Promise?" he asked in an even hoarser voice, giving a nervous giggle that exposed his front teeth. Foaming spittle trickled from the narrow hollows that separated the teeth from one another. His eyes flashed with a peculiar light. A crazy sort of look.

"Yes, I promise," I said, lowering the submachine gun to the ground. The tension disappeared from his face, and the hand holding the ax relaxed its grip, until his fingers opened and it fell to the ground with a clang.

"You won't do anything to me?" he repeated his question, still frightened.

"You can go back to your room," I answered gently. He continued looking at me with staring, wide-open eyes. "Go back to base," I repeated patiently. "Sasson will go with you."

He began walking carefully, rocking on his feet, toward me, as if he was afraid I was going to break my promise. When he and Sasson walked away from me, Shimon's steps broke into a panic-stricken run. I stood where I was, leaning against a pine tree, waiting until they disappeared. By this time I was quite certain he was out of his mind. I returned to my room, depressed and tired. But before I'd had a chance to sit down, there was a knock on the door and Sasson entered. "I took him to my room," he said sadly. "He fell asleep."

"We'll have to take him to the clinic. His nerves have gone. He's going to be pretty useless, I'm afraid."

"Yes, I think he needs a doctor. Maybe even a hospital," Sasson sighed bitterly. He added ruefully: "We've already taken one of our men to the clinic today, and now we'll take another one. He won't return to the front in a hurry. If we go on losing men at this rate, there'll soon be no one left."

"A lousy situation," I agreed. My voice was gruff, and I felt an irritating itching on my scalp.

"And they still call this a quiet part of the front," Sasson scoffed. "God help us where it's busy!"

"I suppose we'd better call the orderly," I said reluctantly.

Sasson was silent for a while. Then he said: "I don't know if it's a job for Yosef. He's still a kid, you know. Only sixteen. He faked his papers and got called up earlier than he was due." He stopped for a moment, giving me a pleading look. "Do you know what he did yesterday?" he asked.

"Well, what?"

"Took a catapult and went off to hunt pigeons. Nearly went into one of the mined areas in the forest. I'm telling you, he's just a kid."

"You're really exaggerating." I stood firm. "I'm not asking you to transfer a load of dynamite."

"If you want me to, I'll call Yosef. But I could really take Shimon there myself. What do you care?"

"No," I said firmly. "Call Yosef. That's his job." Sasson nodded sulkily and went out.

In several minutes he came back, with Yosef following in the rear. I surveyed him closely, hoping to find out something about him from the expression on the face and his movements. He stood carelessly. His face was pale and creamy, and his short body was somewhat slumped. A cigarette was stuck awkwardly behind his ear. His shirt was stained with the blood of his last patient.

The stains had clotted and become dark brown.

"Why's the cigarette behind your ear?" I cross-examined him.

"Because I'm going to smoke it!" he smiled. I laughed.

"And why don't you change your shirt?" I asked in a friendly way.

"Oh, nonsense," he replied, dismissing my remark with a gesture.

"I want you to take Shimon to the first-aid station."

"Right." Yosef smiled back.w

"He's suffering from shock."

"You mean he's a bit mixed up," Yosef corrected me.

"He was always a rather nervous fellow," Sasson intervened. "Always got excited about bugs, lizards, and rats, things like that." He stopped for a moment and laughed to himself. "How were we supposed to know that something like this would happen to him?"

"I saw him when he ran away with the chopper," Yosef said good-humoredly. "I'll take him to the first-aid station. Where is he now?"

"In Sasson's room." Yosef bade us farewell with a careless, unconcerned gesture, as if he was saying: "Don't worry. Leave it all to me. It'll be alright." He went off.

"What's the time?" I asked Sasson. He glanced at his wristwatch.

"Five to one."

"Well, let's go to the dining room and see what things look like over there."

We went off toward the slope, reaching the protective wall with leaps and hops. We went inside and stopped next to the small radio set that stood behind the wall. It was tuned to an enemy radio station. Several soldiers clustered around it. Despite the earsplitting static, the Arab announcer's muffled voice could be heard quite clearly. A hoarse male voice speaking stumbling, guttural Hebrew. "Citizens of Jerusalem," the voice called in a wheedling tone, "why do you want to die of hunger? Your city is besieged. The Arab forces are about to conquer it any day. Surrender! Surrender to us . . ." Sasson put his hand out and switched the set off.

"You should go off to deepen the foxholes," he tongue-lashed the soldiers.

"Go and dig now?" one of the men called out bitterly. "That's just what the snipers want, that we should show ourselves in the open."

"That's exactly why you have to deepen the foxholes," Sasson rebuked him. The soldiers stumbled out complaining and mumbling to one another.

Sasson was in a bad mood. "It's better for them to do some digging than to sit around listening to enemy broadcasts," he snapped angrily. "You know," he added, "stupid as those broadcasts are, they eventually take effect and get into one's head. Yes, it's really better for them to dig foxholes." He lowered his voice: "At least that'll do some good."

"Excuse me." One of the soldiers came up to us. "I would like to talk to you," he said.

"Alright. What's the trouble?"

"Trouble . . . You know what I mean."

"Well, what do you mean?"

"They . . . my parents and my three small brothers, they're giving me trouble." He stopped for a moment, swallowing his spittle in his emotion. "They told me that they didn't get the payment. You know, the family allowance . . ."

"Yes, yes, I know." I looked at his swarthy face. Two dark, alert eyes. A strong expression. About seventeen, I guessed.

"You see . . ." he began again, as I said nothing.

"Your parents didn't receive the money," I repeated.

"No, they didn't," he repeated sadly. "I'm the oldest son in the family," he went on. His words sucked me into my own memories, which had been subdued by the fighting. Since leaving home I had been cut off from my parents as if a magic wand had divided the thread that bound us. A strange process of forgetfulness tore me away from the experiences of the past, from memories of childhood, of my parents. All these had disintegrated and sunk into a hidden corner of my consciousness. Now everything was aroused again. When I thought about my parents now, a shock went through me, as if I'd suddenly discovered their existence for the first time. Were they alright? Worry pinched my heart.

"I'll check with the company office," I told the soldier. I tried desperately to prevent recalling the slumbering memories. But I couldn't suppress them. Now I felt deeply miserable.

"But it's my duty," the soldier persisted. "I've got to bring something home. They need food." Food! The word hammered against my temples like a heavy ramrod shattering what remained of my peace of mind. I was grateful—grateful to this seventeen-year-old boy who had reminded me of my duty toward my parents. The image of my father and mother appeared before me, so sharply that I could make out every detail of their faces. I suppressed a pain every time I saw the tiny creases move in the corners of their sad eyes. I realized why I was so filled with fear and concern.

The wrinkles around their eyes were symbols of starvation and poverty. A feeling of inner tension and unrest spread through me.

Sasson, who stood to one side, chimed in. "Maybe we should give him a few tins of canned meat?" he suggested.

"What are you talking about?" I tore myself away from my

private thoughts. "You know we're on strict rations. If we give him some tins, we may have to do the same for others. In the end we won't have any food left at all."

"Yes, you're right," Sasson agreed sadly.

"But what's going to happen to my parents?" the soldier insisted. "What am I going to do?" His voice became more aggressive, demanding almost, as if he sensed how confused and helpless we were. I didn't know what to say to him. My heart felt heavy.

"It'll be alright," Sasson reassured him. "You'll see, it'll all be OK. Now go and deepen the foxholes, Eliezer. We'll talk to you later!"

Eliezer lowered his shoulders and passed his arm through the leather straps of his gun. When he straightened up, the gun was hanging carelessly on his back. His small body seemed as if it was about to buckle under the weight of the heavy gun. But the boy never stumbled. He strode off with heavy, long strides toward his foxhole.

"Do you know him from before?" I asked, when Eliezer had gone.

"Yes, we live in the same suburb of town. Near the Mahane Yehuda market."

"Oh." A short silence.

"You know what?" Sasson renewed the discussion. "You've already been out with us on night patrols . . ."

"Well?" I asked curiously.

"The enemy village opposite us isn't short of food. They've got chickens, sheep—you know."

"What d'you mean?"

"Well, why don't we go out tonight on a patrol and 'confiscate' a lot of food. I'll take along Eliezer and another soldier." Sasson gave me an expectant look.

"Do you know the area well?" I asked hesitantly.

"Like the back of my hand." He looked excited.

His parents were also in difficulties, it occurred to me.

"Well," Sasson pressured me, "what do you say?"

"Were you born here?" I ignored his question.

"Yes, I was born in Jerusalem," he confirmed. An impatient expression spread over his face. He pressed his lips together, as if restraining himself, until two deep clefts of flesh were etched at the point of his chin.

"And what do your parents do?" I asked.

His face went softer. "They are poor people," he mumbled apologetically. "I haven't had an easy time," he went on sadly. "It really wasn't easy. When I was a small boy, I was forced to earn money for food."

"Yes, I also know what it's like," I broke into his flood of words. He gave me an understanding look.

"What jobs didn't I do in order to get a bit of money!" Sasson's face took on a self-satisfied expression. He was obviously proud of the things he'd done when he was a boy. "Once I sold papers on the street. Another time I delivered flowers for a shop. You know, for weddings or to girls. And when this work stopped, do you know what I did?" He gave me a questioning look.

"Well?"

"I picked sabras—prickly pears."

"Sabras?" I asked in surprise.

"Yes. From the wild hedges around Jerusalem. My brother and I were a team. In the beginning we used to get into fights with the Arab kids who lived around there. But in the end we got along alright. Then we went back to Jerusalem and sold the sabras in the streets. I had a good voice, a sort of high-pitched soprano. And I made up a little tune: "Sabras, sabras!""

"Don't think you're the only one who had a good voice." I smiled. "When I was a boy I sang like a nightingale. I sang in a choir. In the synagogue next door. I even dreamed of becoming a famous cantor one day. But, as you see, I never realized my ambition."

"But I bet you never sold sabras," he claimed, goading me.

"No, that's true," I agreed. "But I bought plenty. I like them. Even today."

"I reckon you're right. I used to eat a lot of them myself—when business was bad." We both laughed.

"I see you're quite used to finding food out in the fields."

"Yes, that's true. So why shouldn't I do the same now?"

"Wait until tonight," I said.

He pulled a sour face.

"I want to see what I can arrange with company HQ."

Sasson smiled tolerantly.

"Do you really think that they have a store of food that they hand out to anyone who needs it?" When he saw how embarrassed I was, he added: "You also won't find a bank there. No one in the army is handing out any money. They're a bunch of skinflints."

"We'll see," I muttered absentmindedly, surprised at how soon I had forgotten the thoughts aroused in me by Eliezer's words. Friends, fellow soldiers whom I had just met became faint shadows in my mind's eye. They seemed to have disappeared in a mist of forgetfulness. The only thing I could remember was the expression on my parents' faces—and even this seemed very far away. A certain change had taken place in me. The cells of my brain must have changed into filters that held back and expelled everything I didn't need, so that I could stay at the front without qualms.

Sasson interpreted my meditations as pangs of doubt for having agreed to his suggestion. But the truth was that I didn't have any misgivings about his plan for raiding the enemy village. On the contrary, when I remembered the food convoy at Sha'ar Hagai, a flash of pleasure took ahold of my heart. The abandoned food trucks had been looted and sacked by the enemy: there was no question about that.

Nevertheless, there still remained in me a spark of resistance to the idea. Some sensation that had not yet been filtered out of my brain. But I rejected my own doubts, at the same time affirming that I wouldn't tolerate stealing in easier and quieter times.

I strolled off to company HQ, deep in thought. "Watch out for snipers," Sasson reminded me, noticing my absentmindedness. I waved goodbye to him with the gun I held.

I made my way carefully, keeping my head well down. The smooth rocks and bushes in the fields served as landmarks. A blurring emptiness closed in within my head, shattering my thoughts and making me tired and drowsy. My brain was blank. I walked along mechanically, hardly conscious of what I was doing.

I found the company commander in his room. His face looked even more weary than usual—and I felt sorry for having to bother him.

"There's some trouble!" I shouted.

"What's wrong?"

"You've probably heard about the two wounded men," I said quickly, pleased with myself for having dignified Shimon with the designation of "wounded."

"Yes," he confirmed sadly.

"In addition, there's a complaint about the non-payment of maintenance grants to the family of another man."

"What's his name?" he asked quietly. "I'll check it in Jerusalem." His words had an indifferent tone, as if he didn't care about the whole business and in fact was annoyed I'd brought it up.

"He has parents and three brothers," I added, raising my voice. "It's urgent!"

"Listen," he reprimanded me, "all I can do is find out. But don't expect miracles. I'm only a company commander, not the director of a bank."

"Yes, I realize that." I remembered what Sasson had said.

"I'll let you have the reply in two or three days," the commander summed up. I left the room, disappointed and bitter.

I returned to the outpost fully reconciled to the idea of raiding the village. It seemed to me quite justified. After all, the Arabs were stealing our food, so why shouldn't we steal theirs? In war there is no hesitation about taking the enemy's life. So why should I have any scruples about taking their food?

I ran through the area so plagued by snipers, and dashed behind the defensive wall next to the dining room. Sasson was waiting there.

"Any news?" he asked, wetting his lips with his tongue.

"It's OK," I snapped. My eyes wandered over the empty tables in the dining room. "Take only two soldiers with you," I added, as if remembering something that had slipped my memory. "I think that should be enough."

"Easily," Sasson agreed, his face lighting up.

"And listen," I said suddenly, feeling I had to warn him, "your job is to mine the snipers' building. When you finish this, you can take a slight detour on the way home. Get it?"

"Sure, of course," Sasson confirmed. For a moment it seemed to me that I caught a hint of resentment in his face.

"It would be stupid to send out two patrols on such a dark night," I added apologetically. "They could easily run into one another."

"That's alright," Sasson reassured me. "We'll do the job. Don't worry."

"Be at the southern fence at exactly ten o'clock," I summed up, feeling once more a burning, nauseous feeling in the pit of my stomach. I knew this wasn't stomach upset, not even a sudden attack of fright. Perhaps it was just weakness, I thought to myself, one hand passing over my overall and pressing my stomach. A dull, discordant rumble came from inside, and I felt even more strongly than before a pinching sensation that contracted my intestines to a single hard mass. *I'll go to the clinic tomorrow,* I decided solemnly, knowing in my heart of hearts that I wouldn't.

At exactly ten, Sasson and his two men met next to the fence. "I'm taking Eliezer and Eli," Sasson said, lowering his voice.

"Bad visibility tonight," I pointed out. He didn't reply. I glanced at their shadows, which were jumping up and down because the soldiers were stamping about trying to keep warm.

"Cold . . . cold," one of them said, teeth chattering. I looked up at the sky. It was dark, with many stars. A cold night. There might be frost.

"Well, are we going out?"

"Have you got hand grenades and steel wires?"

"Yes." Sasson bent over and picked up the kit bag lying at his feet. He lifted it gingerly, placing it on his shoulder with great care.

"Do a good job," I tried to encourage him. "We've got to finish them off. Else they'll finish us."

They nodded in agreement.

"It'll be OK," Sasson assured me.

My eyes, which had become accustomed to the dark, examined the shadow cast by Sasson's sturdy body. He rubbed his hands together in front of his face, and breathed warm air into his clasped palms. "Brrr!" he exclaimed. The dark cap that covered his forehead, head, and ears emphasized the light in his glistening eyes.

"Go ahead," I said to him, putting my foot on the wire of the fence in front of us so that they could pass through the gap. "Come back in about two hours," I whispered. Sasson bent under the low fence, and the others followed in his footsteps. Their receding figures soon became dark shadows, which melted into the darkness. For a moment I could still hear their boots scraping on the smooth stones scattered over the ground.

Then this sound was also swallowed. Night. Silence.

CHAPTER 9

THE FEW

I woke up. Frost and darkness surrounded me. An inner unrest stirred nervousness, made my heart beat faster. The hill . . . snipers . . . from somewhere far away a sound of shooting cracked in my ears, sinking and losing itself. Confused scenes of battle flashed through my mind like lightning. A humming sound? A feeling of swelling and puffiness in my lips. A harsh dryness burned them, until they lost almost all sensation. I rose from my seat and took up the rifle, which suddenly seemed heavier than usual.

With weary, sleepy steps I went out to the post that looked out on the hill. It was just before dawn. The sentry on duty spotted me. "So early?" He sounded sleepy. I muttered something he didn't understand. He didn't ask any more questions, and rubbed his frozen hands against one another briskly and uttered a few words critical of the weather. I came closer to the lip of the outpost.

The night, which was coming to an end, began looking lighter. The dark sky became grayer. Soon the margins of the sky became brighter, and a latticed strip of red spread like a thin thread over the peaks of the mountains. The light continued rising until it enveloped the whole sky and the morning light dominated the scene. It hung in the heavens, as if reluctant to depart, but at last it was also forced out and the sun began to rise. First it just peeked the top of its head out, but soon afterward its whole round shape appeared, like an orange-colored ball of fire.

The color of the sun slowly became a blinding yellow, and I had to turn my eyes away. But it didn't feel warm yet. Time crawled at an irritatingly slow pace. I grew impatient. Skeptical thoughts crept into my head and stayed there. Doubts. *Could we polish off the snipers? Would Sasson's mines work?* My doubts didn't last long. I heard, coming from the valley, a heavy explosion, as if a barrel's spokes had burst. Whitish smoke burst through the cracks in the windows of the house. The valleys around returned the echoes of the loud explosion. The thunder died down, and the smoke floated away and merged into the sky.

"Well, it worked OK," I called out to the soldier standing next to me.

"Hundred percent." He nodded in satisfaction. While talking, he turned his gaze on me. A relaxed, reassured expression spread over his unshaven face. From afar I made out Sasson, coming down the slope toward us.

"Well, wasn't it terrific?" he asked jokingly, when he joined us.

"Boy, you're really first-rate," I agreed, slapping him on the back. "You're a great guy." He was pleased with himself. "How did the patrol go?" I enquired.

"Don't ask," he sniggered. "We had some bad luck. We went into the courtyard of some old dame's house. She opened her mouth and let us have it in a voice like a foghorn. She nearly had the whole darn village after us. 'Shut up, you old hag,' we shouted to her in Arabic, but she only screamed louder. 'If you don't give us a chicken, we'll kill you!' Eliezer threatened her. But the old bitch didn't give us a thing. She just stood there and yelled at us: 'You want to take my chickens! You mongrels! They are my children, my eyes.'"

"So what did you do?"

"Well, naturally we got out of there as fast as we could. We couldn't shoot her . . . After all, she was pretty old," he added, as if justifying himself.

"Better luck next time," I comforted him. His large brown eyes glistened with a sheen of disappointment.

"If you want to," I added, trying to appease him, "you can go out tonight again."

He nodded. "There're no cigarettes." He seemed anxious to change the subject.

"What can I do about it? Smoke the stalks of the grass."

"Anyway, we'll have a little rest from the snipers today."

A series of staccato explosions, a succession of thunderclaps that were swallowed up in one another's echoes, broke into our conversation. I glanced toward Jerusalem. The shelling had begun.

"Speak of the devil . . ." Sasson laughed.

"As soon as it seems like we've been rid of the rifle shots, they start using cannons on us."

"Well, I'm going to sleep," he remarked in an indifferent tone. "I hardly slept a wink last night." He waved in farewell and climbed upward, turning his head around as if taking a last look at Jerusalem. I followed his tired movements until he vanished behind the ridge.

Jerusalem. My eyes wandered over its steep slopes and hill, with their long ridges. Mushrooms of white smoke rose above the roofs of the houses and scattered slowly into the air. The banks of clouds that remained here and there were squeezed against one another, until they joined to form a larger white cloud hanging above the dots of the houses and the woods. And then I felt suddenly that there was a beauty I had not sensed before in the landscape of the city. It was as if my eyes had been opened and I was seeing everything more clearly. It was the first time I had felt a strong affection for Jerusalem. I sensed a hidden bond that tied me to it.

My eyes wandered on, looking for the sources of the enemy shelling. From the olive groves near Bethlehem, tongues of flame flickered out. They flashed against the spots of shadow between the trees, disappearing in the spaces of the valley separating Bethlehem from Jerusalem. I tried to work out the time that had elapsed between the first flicker and the sound of the shell hitting Jerusalem, at the same time wondering whether it would land in the city.

I was nearly carried away by a powerful urge to be in the shelled city. To walk along the streets with their narrow pavements, to look at the rough blocks of stone from which the houses were built. And the skies—which had once seemed so low that they pressed against the densely-packed buildings—now soared up to the heavens. The city had shrunk below the heightened background, showing as a narrow strip with many spikes—the spires of the churches, which seemed to want to pierce the canopy of blue stretched so tautly above them.

My thoughts were interrupted by a soldier who was running along waving his arms anxiously. I couldn't hear him. As he came closer, panting for breath, he spat at me: "Reuven's hurt. A mine."

"A mine?" A wave of heat flooded my cheeks and forehead, spreading to my whole body in a burning, stinging stream. "Where?" I tried to keep calm, to hide my concern. But I couldn't. I could hardly hear myself speak, so soft was my voice.

The soldier pointed toward the wood north of the outpost. "We never dreamed there was anything . . ."

"What about him?"

"Eliezer took him out. He's in first aid."

"Eliezer?" I held the word back for a moment in order to recover from the shock. Mine? My body became hard with fright. I could hardly move my legs. "Hold on a moment," I stammered. "I'll take along the maps of the minefields. We'll go there right away."

"OK," the soldier said. It was obvious he wasn't very keen to go back to the place.

We went off a minute or two later. The shelling of Jerusalem continued, accompanying us as a distant echo. We reached the barbed-wire fence in front of no-man's-land.

"Where?" I asked.

"On the other side of the fence. In the wood."

We bent beneath the fence and went through.

"This is still no-man's-land, isn't it?" I questioned him, my eyes on the map.

"Yes."

"Well, why did you come here?" The soldier shrugged his shoulders. I stopped asking questions. Crossing no-man's-land was a daily occurrence. It meant taking a shortcut and saving time. We stopped for a moment. I broke the branch of a tree, intending to use it as a prod so I could search for mines.

"Is it far from here?" I asked

"About another fifty meters."

The presence of the mines made my head spin. My heart beat like a drum with fear. I breathed heavily, dripping sweat. Slowing down my steps, I poked the rod over the places where I was about to place my feet. We crawled along, feeling dizzy.

"About another twenty meters," the soldier whispered.

I went on feeling my way forward, until I stopped. I smelled a strange smell, and sniffed in curiosity. A kind of dry coolness burned the inside of my nostrils. Stink. A strong, pungent stench that smothered the pine trees' fragrance. It came from a clearing in the wood, where the trees seemed to thin out. I set off for the place where the smell was coming from, and then stopped halfway. In the center of a small forest clearing lay the corpse of a man, flat on his back. The clothes that covered the body were torn, as if they'd been ripped by an iron comb and torn into strips. All the same, I could tell by the clothes that he was an enemy soldier. I saw a face terribly swollen, with a shiny, dark red color, like a reddish apple that had gone overripe and rotted. His neck was also swollen and bulged out, like a dark red roll nearly as big as his head. What was left of a stomach showed through the torn clothes. Its flesh was torn and sliced up, a jagged hole from which his guts stuck out like thick worms. The stink almost made me vomit.

"He must've been here a few days," I gasped, holding my breath because of the smell.

"He's been eaten by jackals."

"Yes." I moved back a few steps. "We'd better get out of here." I went on stepping back, carefully. "There might be some more mines lying about," I added in a choked voice.

"OK." The soldier breathed air into his lungs with relief.

The tracks our feet had left led us back. We left the wood and returned behind the defensive wall next to the dining room. A group of soldiers was busy cleaning their rifles.

"There's a message for you," one of them called out to me. "From company HQ."

I tore the envelope open and drew out a folded piece of paper. Some instinct told me it was bad news. I read the few lines rapidly, greedily, so fast I skipped over the words.

"Well?" the soldier asked.

"Our unit's being reduced again." I was angry. "By another three men. All only sons. Get it?"

He went on staring at me, nodding his head to show he understood. "So there'll only be nine of us," he summed up. The idea seemed to scare him.

"Well, go and call them." I was furious and didn't care who knew it. He peered curiously at the order I held in my hand. I pushed it at him.

"Read the names. And tell them to come here right away. With their things."

He took the order and moved off slowly toward the outpost. From far away, I heard him calling out the names of the soldiers on the list. About ten minutes later, all three of them turned up. They gathered around the camp table on which the transmitter stood, putting their kit bags down on it.

"Well, you're leaving," I said curtly. "Go to company HQ. From there they'll take you back to Jerusalem. You've been released from service at the front, because you're only sons." They stood with their eyes downcast, as if they had just been reprimanded. "Leave the arms here," I added, trying to sound casual, although I felt anger against them in my heart. We were staying there. And they were going. There were so few of us . . .

"You won't need your guns there," I went on.

The soldiers fixed the butts of their guns in the ground and placed the muzzles one against the other, like a tripod-shaped tent. I felt they were trying to make their movements snappy and brisk. When they finished arranging the rifles, they went back to their places and stood in a row.

"Do we have to go?" one of them asked.

"That's the order I've been given. You aren't running away.

Here, give me the order." I turned to the soldier who had brought them together. He handed me the slip of paper.

"Here," I showed them. "This is it."

"Yes," he confirmed in a dull voice.

"So don't make a fuss. Go off quietly. And good luck to you. We'll probably get someone else in your place." They lifted their kit bags rather hesitantly and began walking away with small, tentative steps, as if they were stealing away.

I remembered Reuven. I'd have to visit him in the hospital. A miserable mood had taken hold of me. Within a few days the number of soldiers in our unit had dropped to nine. The thunder of the cannons shaking Jerusalem reminded me that we had no artillery. *What's going to happen?* I thought to myself. *What's going to happen?* I went off to company HQ.

Gershon, the driver, stood next to the armored car, fiddling with the engine. "Well, are we going?" he asked, when he saw me.

"Yes, to Jerusalem . . . to visit Reuven."

He nodded, and we climbed inside. "You see," Gershon said, with a gesture of dismissal, "those young fellows, that whole bunch, don't know what it is to be careful." He gave me an accusing look, as if to say, "You're just the same," then continued, "The army isn't a joke. It isn't the Boy Scouts."

"You're right," I humored him. Gershon drew his finger across his narrow mustache, as if he wanted to comb it. His face expressed satisfaction. He got on my nerves. Gershon always tried to create the impression that he was an expert who knew everything about anything. He was always right. Maybe this was because he was older than most of us and thought he was more experienced.

"In the British Army, where I served," he went on, "they knew what it was to be careful!" He began telling some of the old yarns we had all heard so many times, without bothering to notice whether I was listening or not. We stopped next to the gate of the hospital.

"Wait here for me," I said. "I'll be back in half an hour." I took the two packets of cigarettes I'd brought along, and went out.

The corridor was crammed with dozens of old heavy beds collected from people in the city. Mattresses crowded the whole length of the walls. Everywhere I looked I saw wounded men. In the wards, quick looks, eyes peering around. Patients hoping for visitors peered out of the ward. A smell of carbolic acid in the air, the suffocating smell of ether and the sour stink from the pus of the wounds.

I stopped on the threshold of the first ward and glanced inside. In the dim light two large black eyes shone out. A stabbing look, like the blade of a dagger. Fear. Despair. The sign of approaching death.

"I don't want to live." His eyes penetrated me.

A cold shudder passed through me.

"I don't want to live," he yelled again, making an effort to take in a little air.

A hoarse rattle broke from his tortured lungs, followed by a shrill whistle. Beads of sweat covered his taut forehead and sunken cheeks, as if they were the blisters of a malignant disease. The nurse who stood nearest to him took up a wet towel and wiped his face.

"Water . . . water," his lips spluttered, moving and twitching in torment. When he didn't get what he asked for, he went on screaming: "To die . . . I want to die."

The nurse glanced at me for a moment. I lowered my eyes to the floor, without knowing why I did so. Drops of blood dripped down on the floor slowly, drop by drop, from the mattress. *How long will the blood go on dripping?* I wondered to myself. *How many drops of blood are there in a man's body?*

I remembered the question Yoram had asked in the ruined building at Sha'ar Hagai: "How much blood is there in a man's arteries?" No, it was Yosef, the driver, and not Yoram... Yosef... How many drops?

The nurse's voice broke into my thoughts. "Are you a friend of his?" she asked.

I glanced away from the pool of blood and met her tender brown eyes.

"No, I don't know him," I replied.

"We don't even know his name," she sighed. Her face looked tired. She walked over to the end of the bed.

"Is he going to die?" I asked.

"Yes, I'm afraid so. Both his legs have been amputated, and his stomach has been torn to pieces . . . A mine." She nodded her head sadly.

"So why don't you give him some water? Why is he suffering so much?"

"Do you think I know why? He's going to die. But we're not allowed to give him water. Doctor's orders . . ." Her words were interrupted. A man with a white face and a long silver beard came up to the bed. He stopped at the wounded man's head and looked at him with his warm brown eyes.

"God," the wounded man cried out, "let me die." His lips quivered. Large tears oozed out of the corners of his eyes. He was crying.

"My son," the old man said, bending over him, "God won't hear you." He took a handkerchief in his hands and wiped the tears that streamed onto the dying man's cheeks. "No, he won't hear you."

"God," the dying man went on in his rasping voice, like a broken echo lost in a deep chasm. "God . . ."

"My son," the old man begged, holding back his tears, "don't ask God to commit a sin. Don't ask such a thing." He lowered his head to the dying man's white, almost lifeless hand, and pressed his lips against it gently. His tears wet the dying man's white, shriveled skin, giving it a momentary flash of life.

"Is that his father?" I asked the nurse.

"No," she replied, in a choked voice. "He's a rabbi who comes here every day." She stopped for a moment, wiped her nose with a handkerchief she took out of the pocket of her blue overall, and went on: "He doesn't eat and doesn't sleep. Just goes up and down between the beds and prays for the wounded boys." Her glance combed the rows of beds squeezed close to one another. "And for those who have no relatives, he becomes a father. You can see what I mean."

"Yes, I can see."

"All I know is that if there are any saints in this world, he's one of them."

The old man continued bending over the bed. His tears fell on the creases of the sheet that was stained with the clotted blood of the soldier's body. I looked down at the floor. The drops of blood were still oozing through the mattress. The rattling breathing grew louder, and his eyes opened wide in fear. The rattle turned into a sad, despairing whistle, which became fainter and weaker until it stopped altogether. Only his glassy eyes seemed to go on living. He was dead. He'd gotten what he'd prayed for. I stepped back, hearing his last wheezing breaths still echoing in my ears.

"God has taken him," the old man whispered, still holding the boy's hand and muttering a silent prayer.

"Are you a relation of his, my son?" he asked me in surprise, as if he hadn't noticed me until then.

"No, no," I stammered. "I'm looking for a friend of mine . . . a friend."

"What's his name?"

"Reuven."

"And his surname?"

"Ben-Shalom."

"My son," he said, coming up close to me. He took my hand in his, as if anxious to prepare me for bad news, and looked straight into my eyes. "God has taken him as well. I was there when he died." For a moment I was stunned. Reuven—dead?

Silence.

"Did he suffer like that before he died?" I forced myself to ask.

There was no reply. I looked at the rabbi's large eyes, at his white beard, his face so full of dignity. He didn't try to avoid my gaze, but looked straight at me. His eyes were still damp with tears.

"Did he suffer like that?" I asked again. He maintained his silence, as if he hadn't heard my question.

"May God watch over you," he said suddenly, going out.

I followed him with my eyes. He walked between the beds, holding a Bible in his hand. Walking between the wounded men, he bent over them and whispered: "Trust in God! Trust in God!" Some of them answered by nodding their heads, and others groaned in pain.

After the rabbi left the room, I turned to the nurse. "I'm going to the base," I mumbled. I felt warm and comfortable in her presence.

"Going already . . . ?" Her eyes rested on me.

"Goodbye," I said with a choked voice. "Take these cigarettes," I added shyly. "I brought them for Reuven . . . You can
hand them out among the wounded men." My eyes fell on her
full lips, which were trembling a little.

"Shalom," she said softly and tenderly.

I wanted to go on looking at her, to come close to her, but
the barrier of death was between us. Glassy eyes. The dead man
. . . If fate had brought us together in another place, at another
time . . . If only . . . Fatigue overtook me. A heavy fatigue. Perhaps
the day might come when I would meet her again. We might
become friendly. I went out into the courtyard slowly, dragging
my feet behind me with an effort. Outside, the sounds of shells
exploding shattered the air. The shelling of Jerusalem was still in
full swing.

I climbed into the armored car clumsily. Gershon wasn't in
the driver's seat. Where the devil was he? That was all I needed:
to be stuck there.

After I'd waited for about ten minutes, he came back.

"Where were you?" I asked angrily.

Gershon slouched under the window of the armored car
and gave me a scorching look: "I went for a piss," he remarked
casually.

"Oh," I replied in a softer tone, "not a bad idea. Hold on a
moment. I'll do the same." I went away from the armored car, in
the direction of the nearest open space.

I passed through the gate of the building, which was made
from bars of iron. There was a sound of faint weeping. I stopped
and turned toward the sound. A little girl ran toward me. "Come
here," I called out, walking toward her. She stopped, gave me a
pleading look, and ran to me, sobbing bitterly.

"Soldier, soldier," she cried, "are you my uncle?"

"Yes, of course," I stroked her hair, which was tied with a colored ribbon, as she put her tear-stained face next to my leg. I bent down and took her in my arms.

"What's your name?"

"Shula," she stammered in a voice choked with tears.

"How old are you, Shula?" I asked. She stopped crying.

"Five and a half."

"And where do you live?"

She lifted her head from my shoulder and pointed with her finger.

"And where's your mother?"

"Mummy was frightened by the bomb that went boom . . . It fell in the house. Mummy won't talk to me. I was in the other room when I heard a funny noise. I ran to Mummy, but she wouldn't talk to me . . ."

She couldn't finish, and burst into tears again.

"Don't cry," I tried to soothe her. She stopped weeping and dried her eyes. "And where's your daddy?"

"Daddy's working in the war. He's not here."

"Come, let's go to your home," I suggested. She nodded her head in agreement, and we started toward the place where she said she lived. We walked quickly down the empty lane until we came to a small double-storied house, surrounded by a garden with fruit trees.

"Here it is." Shula pointed. Here was a shattered tiled roof, which gave off a whitish smoke. Taking her in my arms, I walked inside and put her down in the corridor.

"Wait there, Shula," I told her. "I'm going to see where your mother is."

"Alright," she agreed, sitting down on the steps obediently. I ran up to the second story. The door was open, and I walked into a room where the furniture was upside down and thrown about by the shrapnel from the shell that had come inside.

On the floor lay a woman with clasped hands, quite motionless. I bent over her. She was dead. No doubt about that. Strange, but there wasn't a single drop of blood flowing from her body.

"Anyone here?" I shouted. No reply. I ran through the other rooms quickly. When I didn't come across a living soul, I went back to Shula, who was still sitting on the steps.

"Is Mummy alright?" She looked frightened.

"Your mummy's ill," I lied.

"But I want her," she began wailing.

"She can't talk to you now, I'm afraid." I tried to calm her, but she went on crying.

"Maybe we can ask a policeman to find your daddy?" I proposed, hoping this might take her mind off things. She nodded, to my surprise. I took her up in my arms, and we walked rapidly toward the police station in the vicinity. The policemen gave us questioning looks when we entered, and when she saw them, Shula howled even louder.

"Don't be afraid, Shula," I soothed her, stroking her hair. "They're good uncles. They'll try to find your father."

While she inspected them, as if trying to decide whether they'd really help her, I slipped away from her and told one of the policemen what had happened. "I've got to get back to my unit," I explained.

"Don't worry," the policeman observed in a despondent tone, "we'll look after her."

"I have to go," I told her when I was next to her again.

"No," she wailed, "don't go away, Uncle. Stay with me."

"I'm sorry, Shula, I can't." I tried to look away from her

innocent blue eyes. "I'm also working in the war, like your daddy. Do you understand?" I was ashamed for lying to her and for letting her down.

"Like my daddy?" she repeated, in a questioning tone. And at once she added: "So will you come to see me?"

"Of course, of course." I came up to her and kissed her on her forehead. She looked up at me.

"Really and truly?"

"Yes, of course, Shula!" She kissed me on my left cheek. I stepped away, conscious of the depressed feeling growing inside me, pressing against my heart. I waved goodbye to her, and she waved back with her tiny hands.

I went back to the armored car.

"What a character," Gershon complained. "Thought you'd got lost."

"No, no," I was in a gloomy frame of mind. "I met a little girl . . ."

"A likely story," he laughed. "Must have got hold of some tart or other, eh?" A sly smile spread over his face.

"Don't be silly," I tried to protest. But he persisted.

"Come on, nothing to be ashamed of. What was she like?" He must have seen from my expression that I wasn't amused, because he stopped and said abruptly: "Right, let's go." I half contemplated telling him about Shula, about Reuven's death, the nurse in the hospital. But I wasn't in the mood.

Later on, I told myself. *Later on, I'll tell the boys about it.* Gershon started the armored car, and we began our way back to the outpost.

Outside the windows passed the deserted streets of the city. Here and there someone went by us running along the side of the pavement, as if wanting to cling to the stone walls, where they would be safe from the shells. Everything looked terribly dry. For a moment I thought the houses flashing by were nothing but bare masses of rock. The armored car took a sharp turn at the crossroads. "Careful!" I called out. The electric light pole slid toward us. The brakes screamed shrilly, like the cry of a wounded man . . .

Reuven, I thought of Reuven. *Did he cry out like that in his last moment?* I hardly knew him. *Who were his parents? Who would inform them he was dead?* How dreadful to stand face-to-face with bereaved parents, to hear their cries. My thoughts chased one another, hammering at me, bursting through. My eyes passed over the streets with an empty, hollow look.

"Well, we're here." Gershon's voice woke me up. Evening was almost on us, gray and dull. I left the armored car and ran behind the wall that guarded the dining room. Sasson stood next to the radio set, looking worried.

"What's wrong?" I asked.

"We're leaving."

"Who said so?"

"The company OC was here. While you were away. We're leaving tomorrow morning."

"What difference does it make?" Gershon asked. He'd come out of the driver's cabin. "That's a soldier's life," he added philosophically. "Here today, and gone tomorrow."

"Why don't you go pack your things?" Sasson snapped.

"The OC is always right," Gershon hissed venomously, and went off.

"Just a big talker." Sasson was annoyed by Gershon's parting words. He turned toward me, as if expecting me to confirm his last remark. I didn't react. "He likes farting with his mouth," he continued accusingly.

"Did the company commander say where we're being sent to?" I asked, ignoring his other remarks.

"To Sha'ar Hagai." He breathed deeply. "Things aren't too good over there."

"Do the boys know already?" My heart beat with excitement. I felt weak.

"Yes," Sasson giggled. "They all took the news well . . . apart from Benny. He's trying to pull a stunt on us. Claims he has a stomachache. But he won't have any luck with me. I know those stunts."

"Are we being attached to any special unit?"

"The company commander just said: 'You're being transferred to Sha'ar Hagai!'"

"I hope he doesn't expect the nine of us to take the place?" I laughed. Sasson didn't answer. "Right," I went on, "so we'll go there. Do we have a choice?" But my expression showed I wasn't very happy about it. And Sasson couldn't conceal his misgivings either.

"You remind me of my old platoon commander." He tried hard to make his words sound light. "He always used to bark at us: 'There's no alternative,' 'We've no choice,' as if he wanted to get it into our heads that we had to obey his commands. Who refuses? They tell us to go, so we have to go. That's all."

"Yes," I agreed, "you're right. We have to go."

"Well, let's go and pack our things," Sasson suggested. "We're leaving at five." He paused. "Know what? I'm going to carve my name on one of the trees in the forest. They say it's lucky." We walked together through the forest toward the huts on the slope of the hill. "And how's Reuven?" Sasson asked casually.

"Dead," I spat out quickly, as if trying to get rid of the word.

"What . . . what are you talking about?" Sasson was thunderstruck. He remained rooted to the spot.

"Better not tell the others," I said sadly. "It'll crush their morale."

"You're right . . . Quite sure about it?" he asked, as if he couldn't believe Reuven was dead.

"Yes," I confirmed. We walked on without speaking, in the direction of the forest. Suddenly the little mound over the enemy soldier's grave appeared before us. The stick we'd put in it had fallen down, and the sad-looking heap of earth was covered with broken branches and yellow autumn leaves. We stole away from the place and made for the slope. Through a disused communication trench we came to an outpost looking over the gray hollow of the valley. We gazed at it somberly, without speaking. Night fell. A strange silence hung in the air around us. Even the dogs in the village opposite seemed to have their tongues tied to their mouths.

"So quiet," Sasson whispered. "As if there wasn't a person there."

His voice died down. He shuddered all over. I was worried about him. He used to be so cheerful and cocky.

"Why don't you get some sleep?" I suggested. "You look tired."

"No, no. I can't. I'll stay here." He looked at me. "Maybe you should take a nap. It won't do you any harm."

"OK. I'll relieve you in the second shift."

I went off toward the huts. Through the dark windows came the sounds of soldiers talking as they packed for their journey the next day. I stopped, trying to catch the muffled voices through the wood.

Someone shouted in a loud voice, and others laughed.

I came closer, and heard Eliezer's raucous voice: "It's going to be hot over there in Sha'ar Hagai . . . Yeah, really hot." His voice sank, and then rose to its usual high pitch. "I'm fed up with this place. Sitting on our arses in this bloody hole . . . I want some real action . . ."

"What do you expect in Sha'ar Hagai—roses?" Shabtai went for him.

"He's right," a third voice chimed in. I didn't recognize it. "The situation down there is lousy. They say the Arabs are going to finish off Etzion Bloc."

"Rubbish," Eliezer snorted. "Our people always say things are bad, that we've got our backs against the wall. You know as well as I do that it's all propaganda. They don't want us to get slack . . ."

"You're talking shit," the third voice snapped.

Eliezer laughed contemptuously. "Boy, you're a real defeatist. You've been listening to too many Arab broadcasts."

"Let's wait and see who's right."

"And I tell you that we'll finish them off at Sha'ar Hagai," Eliezer declared boastfully. "We'll have no trouble there!"

"You're a great hero, aren't you?" the third voice went on doggedly. "Haven't you heard about Pine Hill? Right there, at Sha'ar Hagai?" No one answered. "They wiped out our whole unit there. Not once, but twice."

"Rubbish," Eliezer heckled him. "We'll squash them like flies."

"OK, take it easy," Shabtai tried to calm him down. "We won't stop you. Besides, we know you like flies." He sniggered.

"Yeah," Eliezer echoed, in a cheerful voice. "You mean the game we played at Atarot?"

"Let's hear about it," the other soldiers chorused.

"You see," Eliezer explained, "we were on guard duty at Atarot. And it was pretty boring, I can tell you. So we invented a game: the chariot game. We used to catch flies and tie their wings with thread. Twenty or thirty at once." He stopped and laughed loudly. "Then we tied the threads to an empty matchbox. The matchbox was the chariot, you see, and the threads were the reins. We had races. The flies pulled the chariots along, and we took bets on which one was going to win."

"And then?" a curious voice asked.

"Then we threw all the flies to the ants. They used to eat them. Slowly. Eating them alive . . ."

"Sickening. Imagine someone did that to you?"

"It was just a game," Eliezer tried to defend himself. "Just a lark. Only meant in fun." One of the men laughed. And a muffled voice whispered something I couldn't hear.

I opened the door of my room and walked over to the bed. Outside I heard a sad voice singing. I couldn't identify it. Such a sad voice:

I have a lake
The Sea of Galilee
When the sun burns bright
It shines like a silver mirror
But at night
It's as dark as my thoughts . . .

Something within me fluttered, was caught tight. Longing for something I wanted, whose meaning I didn't fully understand. What was it? A strange feeling spread through me. My flesh went taut, stopped tingling. I stretched myself out on the bed. A stinging dryness spread over my eyes. A damp warmth trickled through my belly, and a fatigue.

Sleep took hold of me: a restless sleep through which moved troubled visions and dark shapes.

CHAPTER 10

NIGHTMARE

A flat gray field appeared in front of me. Avenues of yellowing trees defined its crescent-shaped borders. The tops of the trees fluttered in a hot, arid wind. Thousands of leaves, flying about in the strong breeze, blossomed in the air like a flock of birds frightened away by the hunters' shots. Everything seemed to be moving around nervously. The trees rocked from side to side, bending backward and forward. Suddenly they seemed to forge ahead. They were coming toward me. Walking . . . Their trunks had sprouted legs. Not real legs, only roots. Swollen, twisted roots to which black soil had stuck like glue. The roots curled around, sliding forward like worms that had smelled food and were making for it feverishly.

I drew back. Fear rang in my ears like the screaming of thousands of sirens. I fled, I sprinted, I ran as fast as I could. Something I couldn't see blocked my path: a cold barrier, something frozen, which threw me to the ground when I ran headlong into it. I raised my head to see what was happening. One of the trees stood above me. It stretched out its winding legs and pulled me to the ground. I gazed up at it in despair.

The tree had a wizened face—and eyes. This frightened

me more than anything. Thousands of eyes hidden among the shadows of the trees, which rustled in dry voices. The tree bent over me with flexible movements and held out its arms. The dried-out, withered wood caressed me. I was lifted into the air and carried away, struggling and kicking to free myself. But in vain. I was caught, trapped.

"Where are you taking me to?" I cried out in despair. "Where . . . ?" But there was no reply.

Only the whistling of the wind.

"Leave me alone," I screamed so loudly that the roof of my mouth was scorched. "I don't want to leave here!" The tree went on its way, and I screamed louder.

I had no more strength left. My hands lost their grip and fell helplessly. Tears streamed from my eyes, large, heavy tears that dripped onto the field below me. The drops sank into the ground, making round, glistening pools. My head fell downward with fatigue, and when I looked behind me, my eyes met an endless row of these pools. The tree stopped moving. Beneath me a great abyss yawned, like a dark, waterless sea, a hollow sea without a bottom. The tree bent over the abyss and threw me into it with a vigorous motion. My body contracted in fear, and I put a hand out in front of me in an attempt to take hold of one of the branches. But it was too late. The abyss swallowed me up. I fell right into it, diving into its infinite depths, diving down, deep down.

Dizziness circled in front of my closed eyes. A black whirlpool raced and spun. My insides were torn out of me, as if they wanted to leave my body. Suddenly this stopped, and the feeling of nausea was removed as if by a magic hand. Was I imagining this feeling of relief?

I opened my eyes a little, as if I couldn't believe what I'd experienced. But I couldn't see anything. A pleasant shudder ran through my eyebrows and made them dance up and down. A languorous feeling swept through my body, like the delight of quenching a long thirst. A delightful smell wafted in the air breathed in by my lungs. The smell grew stronger. I breathed it in, drew as much of it into my lungs as I could. It was so ineffably sweet, as if I knew every breath was to be my last.

A scent of perfume. The perfume of flowers, of citrus and orange blossoms. The perfume of blossoms at the height of their scent. It fused with my blood, penetrated to every cell in my body, trickled into the marrow of my bones, swept into my head. Intoxication.

My limbs lost their weight and hovered like feathers in the wind, flying about gaily and frivolously in the air, being carried upward. I had no wings, but I was flying . . . flying . . . flying in the air. I was so light, and I felt so good, so happy.

My vision also came back to me. I blinked my eyes. Now I could see a colored mist, a mist made up of blue, yellow, and red clouds, which washed and melted into one another.

Like the brisk movements of a swimmer, my hands beat like oars on the surface of the misty waves. I swam in the mist. The touch of the waves was smooth and tender.

They gave off a melting warmth, which confused my senses until I didn't know what I was doing, so relaxed and pleasant did I feel. A wind as soft as silk, warm and mild, blew in my face. My hair blew wildly over my forehead. I stretched my hand out in order to smooth it down, to straighten it, but it fled from the touch of my hand, ran away, escaped, went wild again, and flew about all over my forehead and to the sides. I tried again and again, but my hair wouldn't stay in one place.

The colored mist beneath me thinned out a little, spun out, opened up. Through its narrow channels appeared a dark sky, the color of the sea, in which thousands of stars glittered. A fat, round star circled slowly in the host of other stars. It came close to me, its pale light giving off a sad glow. In a blurred fashion I realized its color was darker than I had first thought. When it came closer I discovered it wasn't a star at all, but a gray, glistening ball of marble. Its closeness sent a shudder through me, a cool shiver of revulsion. I wanted to get away from it.

I tried even harder to fly away and escape from the place. A sharp sense of terror gripped me. My peace of mind was disturbed. All of a sudden I knew that this ball was the world. The world from which I'd just been expelled. Then why was I running away from it?

I turned my eyes skyward desperately, like a shipwrecked sailor whose raft is sinking.

Thousands of colored bows quivered in front of me, thousands of bows, each holding on to one another's midriff, covered the face of the skies, forming the most beautiful rainbows.

Here's the exit, I thought happily, swimming toward them. But it made no difference, because the bows also rose up. I couldn't reach them, and I sighed sadly when I realized I was wasting my efforts.

Were these bows the gateway to heaven . . . ?

A soporific drowsiness spread through my body, draining the strength from my limbs and organs, making my head droop. Once more I smelled the perfume floating in the air. A sweetish, pleasant taste clung to my mouth, a taste that left a warmth in my mouth, a soft and tender warmth.

Exhausted as I was, I took a sleepy look at the marble ball floating under me. The colored clouds surrounded the ball with a curtained smokescreen, through which it could be seen moving about. A sweet slumber took hold of me.

I woke up some time later, feeling warm and relaxed in my joints. I didn't know where I was. All I knew was that I was floating in the mist. But this time it looked different. Its colors had become faded, without any gloss.

A faint tone came to my ears, from afar, as if it had crossed endless magic plains that had made its notes purer, more refined. Where did they come from? I pricked up my ears and listened. It was a trumpet—a trumpet with a thin sound, almost weeping, lonely, sad, weak. It blared on and on as if it would never stop. I wanted to reach it, to hold the trumpet. But I couldn't. Just to see it, to touch it . . .

A sad thought stole into my heart and upset me: There wasn't a single living being around me, not a human shape. I looked around feverishly, desperately, hoping to discover someone, anyone. But all I saw were colored mists floating on the surface of the black, star-studded heavens. Loneliness. Terror. I shouted out: "Anyone here? Anyone here?"

"Ere . . . ere," echoes came back to me. The syllables, which rained down from all sides, went on reverberating in the infinite space, until they died away slowly. In utter despair I screamed: "Is there nobody? Nobody?"

"Body . . . body . . ." the echoes said.

Everything became red. The mist was red, and so were the bows. And the skies were like the ripped-open belly of a giant beast.

"Save me! Save me!" I cried, at the point of tears, closing my eyes in dread. "Oh God! Oh God!"

"Oddd . . . oddd . . ." the echoes answered.

The sound of drums came to me. At first the sound was weak, but it grew stronger until it became the sound of measured beats. I opened my eyes cautiously. Heavy darkness. The colored clouds had lifted. The bows in the heavens were invisible. Only the drums went on beating, hammering. Went on hammering and hammering. The darkness began to retreat as the night gave its place up to the next day. The light grew stronger, until I realized that I stood in a wet field flooded with water, like a soggy swamp. A bubbling sound. I turned my head. A frog as large as a man was coming out of the swamp toward me. Its horny skin was dirtied by the mud, and its eyes burned like two coals of fire.

I stepped back in disgust and horror. The frog didn't take its eyes off me. It raised itself on its hind legs, stretched its front legs out to me with a threatening movement, and opened its wet mouth, from which poured a yellow spit-like pus:

"*Habia . . . habia . . . habia*," the frog croaked in rhythm every time it stretched its feet out toward me. Each time it did this I jumped back, trying to escape its sickening touch. Now thousands of other frogs came out of the swamp and joined the frog who was hunting me. They formed lines, standing firm on their hind legs and holding their front legs out toward me, calling out: "*Habia . . . habia . . . habia.*" It sounded like the groaning of a pump: "*habia . . . habia . . . habia.*" The sound grew louder, maddening, deafening.

Then I understood: I was in the land of the dead. I was dead . . .

The realization of my death didn't come as a shock. I fully accepted it. It wasn't as terrible as I had feared. And if I was really dead, why should I be afraid of the frogs? What could they do to me now?

"I'm not afraid of you," I yelled at them. They stood stock-still on their hind legs. "I'm not afraid!" I screamed. The frogs retreated, and at every step they grew shorter. They went on retreating until they returned to their usual size. I stormed forward, treading them underfoot in a fury of revenge. Jets of blood spurted over my feet when I split their smooth bellies. A thin, weepy voice, like a little girl crying, stopped me. A little frog stood next to my feet: "Don't kill me," it pleaded. "Don't kill . . ." The tone sounded familiar. A faint memory stirred to life in me. I took a step back.

"Can you speak?" I stammered excitedly. The little frog didn't answer. It moved away cautiously, and when it was out of reach of my foot, it sank into the mud and disappeared. The other frogs did the same. Once again I was all alone . . .

The spots of blood on the mud made me feel sick. I wanted to lift my legs and go, but I found they were stuck in the mud, and were getting deeper and deeper. I tried with all my might to extricate myself, but I couldn't. I was sinking, drowning. I held my hands out to the sides. I was unable to move my feet. The mud climbed up my body until it reached my chin and the edge of my lips. My hands, which were stretched upward, froze in place as if caked in the mud and muck that clung to them. Two eagles emerged suddenly out of the black skies. They swooped straight toward my face, letting out shrill cries. Their sharp beaks were aimed at my eyes—and I couldn't move!

"My eyes!" I screamed in horror. "Not my eyes!" I tried to turn my head to one side, to evade the birds of prey that were about to pounce on me. Something hit me on the head.

My hands touched a cold floor. I opened my eyes wide. The shadow of a bed appeared next to me. I was lying on the floor. I must have had a nightmare. I turned my watery eyes to the window, through which came the moon's silver light. Wearily, I lifted myself up from my place, toward the pale light that broke through the window. I could see a black strip of sky studded with stars. The shadow of the iron bars on the window outlined pale squares of light on the opposite wall.

My body was covered by cold, clammy sweat. I wiped my wet forehead with the palm of my hand. Then I picked up the blanket, which was lying on the edge of the bed, and wrapped it around me. I left the room and went outside. Clear skies, decorated with tinsel stars, hung above me like a painted blue canopy.

Dogs yelped in the Arab village. From time to time the wail of jackals cut through the sleepy night air. Occasionally a nervous sentry fired a stray shot. I went forward, to the barbed-wire fence.

"Who's there?" the sentry challenged me.

"It's me." I was eager to hear another person's voice. It was Eliahu.

"Oh . . ." There was a short silence. "Can't you fall asleep?" he asked eventually.

"Yes. But I had a bad dream . . . Thoughts. You know . . ."

"I'm also worried," he said. "Not about myself," he added apologetically. "My brother is in a unit in the Negev. There's fighting down there. I'm anxious about him. I don't know why . . ."

"Let's hope for the best."

"I'm afraid something's going to happen to him," Eliahu went on in a gloomy voice. "We're an unlucky family. My grandfather was killed in the First World War, my father was wounded in the Second World War . . . See what I mean?"

"But why are you so worried about your brother? Why aren't you concerned about yourself?"

"Dunno. Just a sort of feeling, I suppose."

"Where are your parents?"

"Divorced."

"Well, that happens often enough."

"Yes. But not everyone thinks that way. Look at me. I'm taking a girl out. Two years already, and it's serious, but her folks are against it. 'His parents were divorced,' they keep telling her, 'and he won't appreciate you properly.' As if divorce was a contagious disease . . ." He put his hand into his battle dress. "Here, I've got a picture of her. Too bad it's dark now, or else I'd show it to you. She's a lovely girl."

"Show it to me tomorrow, OK?" I said politely. Another silence. "And what does she say?"

"We're going to get married, despite her parents. As soon as I get back from this lousy war. We'll build a house, have some kids . . . Maybe I want it so much because my folks didn't succeed."

"Maybe."

"What about you?" he asked, almost affectionately. "Do you have a girl too?"

"Sure," I lied, afraid of seeming immature. "But it isn't very serious. I mean, I'm not thinking of getting married yet."

"Oh, you still have plenty of time."

"Yes," I agreed, "I'm in no hurry."

But in my heart I felt a burning feeling. When would I also have a girl, instead of having to make one up? And did I really have so much time?

Eliahu glanced at his watch, lifted his head, and said happily: "In another quarter of an hour Hayim will be here to relieve me."

"I'll stay until he comes."

"I think he's here already."

The sound of approaching footsteps. A shadow. Hayim's slouching shape showed itself. He came up to us and waved his hand in greeting.

"You're early," Eliahu chuckled.

"Couldn't sleep. Was sort of restless."

"He has insomnia, too," Eliahu laughed, pointing at me.

"Not really insomnia," I denied the charge. "Just found it hard to fall asleep. I'll try again now."

Eliahu waved goodbye to Hayim. I did the same, and we went off together to the huts.

"He's a good fellow," Eliahu said. "Hayim's as punctual as a clock. Always in time for shift." He slowed down his pace, giving a long yawn. By this time we'd already reached our rooms, and each of us went his own way.

I climbed into bed again, hoping that this time I'd sleep soundly. But snatches of thought, disconnected ideas, bothered me: *What had that dream meant?* The cries of the dying man in the hospital echoed in my ears: "I want to die!" . . . War . . . death . . . The cries of madness in the ruined building at Sha'ar Hagai: "Jews, you're going to die . . ." Death everywhere . . . In a few hours I'd be going back. I might meet the same man again. A dull fear seized me. If only I didn't have to go there. But I knew I'd go, although my whole being was against taking this step. These thoughts flashed through my head until the early hours of the morning, when I fell asleep.

But it didn't last long. Sasson bent over me. "We're moving," he said.

I rubbed my burning eyes. A bitter taste in my mouth. "Yes . . . of course." I felt blank, all clogged up. I passed my hand over my forehead. "I'll soon be ready." I got up and went outside, shivering with cold.

"Going to the war, boys?" The "old men"—aged forty or fifty—smiled, in a feeble attempt to encourage us. They'd been sent to replace us. Someone made a joke at their expense. We all climbed into the armored car.

"All inside?" Gershon asked.

We all shouted: "Yes."

"Then let's go," he said excitedly, as if he wanted to wake up the men sitting half-asleep in their places. No one responded, and the armored car set off. The trip didn't take long. We came to the Schneller camp.

"That's it." Gershon stopped the car next to a stone building. We leaped outside.

The company commander stood on the road, his eyes fixed on us. "Bring your things into the building," he called out to us. Looking at me, he remarked: "Come to see me when you're finished settling in." We took our belongings and arms out of the armored car and made for the building.

A short time afterward I marched toward the headquarters, worried about the fighting that lay ahead of us.

CHAPTER 11

THE ORDER

"You're going out tonight." The company commander's eyes were fixed on me as casually as if he was talking about playing football. "Your job is to take the Pine Hill." The expression on his face changed, and his voice became more earnest. "And it's not an easy job." He stopped for a moment, examined my face, and swallowed his saliva nervously. "You've got to hold the place at any cost. You'll get reinforcements in the morning." He broke off for a moment to ask: "Do you understand?" I nodded. "Armored cars will bring you to the foot of the hill. From there you'll have to walk." I nodded again. His voice became firmer: "Do you follow me?" he asked again, as if waiting for me to agree.

Did we really have to go? Could we refuse?

I nodded my head again, even though something inside me rebelled. No, I didn't want to go. The place we were being sent to was an abattoir. I'd heard all about it. It had changed hands several times already—and each time the men there had come to a bitter end. Now we were supposed to take it. Did we have a chance? Perhaps the whole thing was a terrible mistake?

"Tonight at ten, you'll set off," the company commander

summed up. "Have the men here, in full battle dress." He gave me a grave look. Had he read my thoughts? "Until then you can go out on leave in Jerusalem."

I returned to the building. The men stood next to the door and looked at me. "Well, what's new?" Sasson asked.

"We're going out on a job. Tonight at ten. Until then, we're free. On leave."

"Terrific!" A general outcry of happiness.

Terrific? They didn't know what was waiting for them, and there would be no point in telling them. Let them enjoy themselves while they could.

They began scattering in different directions.

Later on, toward evening, Sasson came up to me: "Are you going to town?"

"Yes."

"Me too. Going to meet my girlfriend." He stopped for a moment, giving me a proud look. "Where're we going to?" he asked while we walked along.

"The Pine Hill."

"The Pine Hill?" Sasson stopped in his tracks. "But that's a death sentence. So they say."

"I know, but someone has to go there. That's how it is."

"I know, I know." Sasson sighed and clenched his lips tight. It was obvious he was trying to keep his nerves under control. "We have no alternative, remember?"

"That's right," I repeated. "No alternative. Maybe we'll have more luck than the others."

An oppressive silence hung in the air. We walked along

without saying a word, taking heart from the fact that we were together. We soon came to the soldiers' club.

"Maybe I'll come in with you all the same," Sasson suggested rather hesitantly.

"No, no," I stammered. "Go to her. Go along." He remained standing outside the club. I patted him on the shoulder and pushed him along. "Don't be a child. Go."

"I'll be seeing you," he said, in a voice full of guilt, as if he was committing a sin by leaving me there.

"See you."

I went inside. The room was crammed with square tables. Happy groups of soldiers sat around them. Someone was playing an accordion with a harsh, grating sound. He played so hard! Why couldn't he put more feeling into it? He put all his emotion into his body, which he twisted around to the rhythm of the music. I found an empty chair for myself. The soldiers sitting around the table glanced at me for a moment and then went back to what they were doing before. Dozens of faces flashed before my eyes. Sunburned, with hair wild and tangled, smiling, laughing, slapping one another on the back the way soldiers do. I didn't know a soul there. Here and there I saw a girl's face—but only a few of them.

How much I would have liked to have a girl there with me. I would have put my head on her shoulder and placed my hungry lips against the hollows of her soft neck. I would have smelled the perfume of her skin. Her hair would cascade over my face, over my burning forehead. Threads of silk, the girl's hair, silken threads . . . The nurse in the hospital! I didn't even know her name. Perhaps I could walk past the hospital and try to meet her, as if by chance. My time was limited. I only had two hours left before we had to leave. Only two hours. I remembered her well.

As if I'd seen her only a few minutes earlier. I felt as if I was in bed at night staring into the darkness. These moments of imagining left a sullen, oppressive feeling in my loins. How beautiful her eyes were. They were pulled a little downward, as if they wanted to join the hollows of her cheeks. If she'd been there with me, I would have caressed her long fingers. They were so graceful and slender that they heated my blood. And what was I to her?

She had probably forgotten all about me. For her, I was only a passing figure, one face among hundreds that moved hazily through the hospital. I wanted very much to see her again. I needed her and longed to have her near.

It would be good to know that someone remembered you. No one remembered me . . . my parents . . . they couldn't have forgotten me . . .

Was there any girl who remembered me? I doubted it. How much I wanted the nurse to sit next to me. I could love her. She would certainly give me a sad, pleasing look, and would beg tearfully: "Don't go, don't go!" Then I'd feel I was a man leaving behind a weeping woman as he went forth to do battle.

Now I was so lonely. I didn't have a soul to talk to . . . The company commander would wait for me at ten o'clock. He would remember me, he would wait for me. His voice was tough, hard. He would focus on his watch and say: "Time to go . . . time to go" . . . Yes, we had to go. But why did it have to be me? I felt I was a nervous, shivery boy—not a man. If only I had a girl of my own.

The rasping sounds of the accordion sawed into my ears. "What's the time?" I asked one of the soldiers sitting next to the table. He turned his face toward me, raised his hand to his eyes, and moved around a little so that he could see his wristwatch.

"Half past eight," he replied.

I got up slowly and made my way through the crowd to the door with measured steps.

I went onto into the pitch-dark street. I began marching along without the faintest idea of where I was going. I didn't want to go back to camp yet. It was too early. Maybe I should just walk past the hospital. I might run into her there. She might come out of the gate at that moment. She'd be surprised to see me, and would fix her soft, gentle eyes on me, asking: "Where are we going?" as if she'd been my girlfriend for a long time.

"Don't ask questions," I'd reply in a mysterious tone—and an understanding smile would spread over her face.

"Some job you can't tell me about. Right?" But I wouldn't answer, and my masculine silence would only confirm her suspicions. "Tonight?" she would pressure me. Her hands would be raised, her long fingers combing my hair. She'd come closer. Then she'd run her fingers across the back of my neck. I would pull her to me until I felt the touch of her flesh against mine. Her head would fall back, her lips would open. I'd bring my lips closer . . .

A strong beam of light fell on me. *Where was I?* I was right beside the hospital. I hurried toward the gates. Next to the entrance stood trucks and ambulances, from which stretchers with wounded men were taken out, carefully, deftly, and carried into the hospital. The headlights of one of the ambulances lit up the pavement near the gate. I walked toward it. Two familiar eyes peered out at me. A strange, unearthly look. I bent over the wounded man. His whole body was covered by a woolen blanket: only his head was exposed.

"Erez?" I called out in surprise, trying to hold back my cry.

"Yes," he groaned sadly, "it's me."

"What happened? Are you badly hurt?"

"Bullets in my leg . . ." He breathed heavily, biting his lips. "Could have been worse, I suppose."

"Painful?"

He nodded.

"Many wounded?"

"Yes. From Sha'ar Hagai."

A cold sweat broke out, covering my face and forehead. "I'm also going there," I told him in a faint voice.

"Really? When?"

"Tonight . . . Hope you get better soon, Erez. They'll look after you here, don't worry."

"Be careful," he groaned. "Just watch your step and you'll be alright."

"Leave him alone," one of the stretcher-bearers rebuked me angrily. "Can't you see we're trying to take him inside?" I turned around to him. He stood next to me, hands on his hips. "Well move along," he snapped impatiently. "And don't waste our time. We have our hands full . . ."

"Goodbye, Erez," I said hurriedly. "And get better soon."

"Goodbye. Be seeing you. Come and visit me."

The stretcher-bearers lifted him up and strode through the gate. His eyes continued to follow me. As he vanished into the darkness, I whispered once again: "Goodbye . . . be seeing you." I could have followed him into the hospital. I might even have met her . . . But it wasn't the right time. I had to go back to base. I began walking back.

The armored car was already standing next to the headquarters building. On the ground stood a shiny new machine gun, with several cases of ammunition and a bag of hand grenades. There was a pungent smell of gun oil.

The quartermaster glanced at me. "You're leaving at ten, right?"

"Yes," I confirmed in a sleepy voice.

"In another half an hour."

"Yes," I agreed without enthusiasm.

"A new machine gun," he went on with an air of importance. "Just arrived." He bent down to pick up the bag of grenades. I joined him, and we placed it gingerly in the armored car. The soldiers began to arrive.

By ten o'clock all of them were there. Each took his gun and sat down in the armored car. There they sat bent and tense over the muzzles, sunk in thought. Sasson remained standing outside. He put in the machine gun and ordered Hayim: "Take the ammunition!" When all the cases were inside he said: "Right, we're ready."

I turned to the driver: "Let's go."

The armored car set out on its way. Dark streets. Blocks of densely packed houses. The distant sound of people singing in chorus. Something tugged at my heart. Who could sing at a time like this? Young boys and girls. They were singing that song about the Sea of Galilee. The one I'd heard before. Everyone seemed to be singing it. A pleasant, melting tune, which became fainter and fainter until it faded into the distance.

The dark landscape visible through the open windows began to change. The shadows of mountains. Sha'ar Hagai wasn't far now. We sat silently in the bumping car. My mind was empty, drained of all thought. Something in me was asleep, dulled, overtaken by an intense sadness. I wanted to close my eyes and forget everything around me.

The car stopped in front of the pumping station. "We're getting out here," the driver broke the silence. We piled outside and removed everything from the car: ammunition, machine guns, and grenades. Sha'ar Hagai. I glanced around me curiously.

The mountain pass looked like a narrow, winding canyon, closed in by giant walls on both sides. Only a thin, clear strip of sky hung above us. A moon as pale as the face of a dead man was suspended at the edge of the heavens, like the heavy, waterlogged prow of a ship sinking slowly into the depths of the ocean.

I had come back to the place where I'd experienced my first taste of battle . . . The convoy. The noises men make when they fight. The ruined building . . . There it was. A black, muffled shadow. Next to it was the hill where I had taken a human life, the life of an enemy, for the first time. I saw once more the image of his hands held out to the sides, like a puppet worked by a spring that had broken.

My attention was caught by rapid steps and the shadow of a man approaching. Someone was coming toward us from the pumping station, waving as he hurried along.

"I'm the scout," he whispered when he arrived. "The company commander sent me here." He stopped for a moment to inhale a deep gust of air. "I'll show you the way to the hill. My name's Yisrael." Without waiting for a reply, he counted the people standing in a row. He pointed his finger at us. "Only nine of you?" he asked in surprise, stopping when he came to me.

"Is that you?" he asked. "Well, don't you remember me?" I glanced at him. A thin face and blond hair.

"Of course," I called out, "of course I do!"

"You remember, in the armored car." He slapped me on the shoulder. "It was me who lifted you up from the floor. Boy, we really got hammered that night."

"Yes, it was no joke." I tried to sound lighthearted. "You seem to like this place. What do you see in it? Can't tear yourself away?"

"Listen," he said suddenly, pulling me to one side and dropping his voice almost to a whisper. "Things are hot up there. See that your men dig themselves in well."

"We'll get reinforcements in the morning," I said with a pounding heart, trying to calm myself. "It's not as bad as you make it out to be . . . Remember what happened in the convoy?"

"Yes, of course." He sounded worried. "But now it's different, more dangerous. They have cannons. You'd better make certain about those reinforcements. Otherwise you don't stand a chance." He said this quite simply, as if stating a fact.

"And what's the situation here?" I asked cautiously.

"The hill itself is free of enemy forces now. They've taken the outposts all around it. Tomorrow morning they'll probably try to reconquer the hill. But first they'll shell you as hard as they can." The dull chatter of machine guns rolled toward us from afar. "They'll attack in the morning. So dig yourselves in well."

"Alright." I tried to assume an air of indifference.

"Well, we've got to get moving," Yisrael urged. "That's where we have to go." He pointed toward the steep, dark slope, and we began climbing up it slowly, feet slipping and sliding over the stones.

"Tougher than I thought," I called out to Yisrael, who was skipping up the hill like a goat. "Slow down a little," I begged him. The winding row of men couldn't keep pace with him.

"Let's take turns carrying the cases," Sasson suggested. "They're damn heavy."

"Alright," I agreed. "Give me the machine gun."

He came closer and handed it to me. We went on climbing. Time crawled by. All of us started showing signs of fatigue. We moved more slowly. Our hands swelled up and grew heavy with the effort of carrying the equipment. The rocks scratched our knees and the palms of our hands, and the summit of the hill still seemed very far away. Streams of sweat poured down me. Its warmth seemed to melt my slack muscles. I went on climbing, moving my head from side to side stubbornly. I had to get there. The summit wasn't far, I told myself. My thoughts were confused. I was pulled downward by a desire to lie on the ground, to stretch myself flat. I didn't give in. But when we reached the top, all of us flung ourselves on the ground, as if by a command.

"Come, I'll show you the lay of the land," Yisrael whispered. "I want to get back to the pumping station before daylight. You've got to watch out for the snipers around here."

"What's the time?" I asked, a little revived. I would have liked to go on pressing myself against the cool earth to draw in some of its lightness, to press my burning cheeks against it, and to rest—to rest without thinking of time. Until the end of the world.

"Three o'clock."

"Already?" I called out in surprise.

"What did you think?" Yisrael retorted. "You climbed up here like a bunch of old women."

"I'm just going with Yisrael to survey the ground," I said to Sasson. "I'll be back in a moment."

We walked to the top of the hill, which was strewn with stones. We surveyed every bush and fence cautiously to make sure the place was really empty. "Not a soul about," Yisrael finally decided.

In front of us the slope stretched away and down. At its end was the blackish shadow of the wood. Far away I saw high ridges that closed us in all around. "Watch the machine guns on that hill, to the right," Yisrael added, catching the glint in my eyes. He gestured to the hill, which was covered with trees. It was only about two hundred meters away. "They bang away from there the whole day. Just never stop. Wait until it's dawn, and you'll see what I mean."

I swallowed my spittle. The muscles of my throat were as hard as stone, and an annoying dryness spread through my mouth. My eyes turned almost automatically, looking for a way to retreat. If only I could have, I'd have gotten up and fled. Run away . . . Where to? In my mind's eye, I could see myself running down the slope. I looked back at Yisrael. What was he thinking? He didn't look alarmed or afraid at all. He was stronger than me. Brave. His silent shadow looked like a black, hard, tough marble statue. Abashed and humiliated, I moved closer to him, so that my shoulder touched his.

"Have you often been up here?" I asked.

"Yes. There's been some hard fighting up here. We lost a lot of men."

"And what about that hill?" my voice was choked as I pointed to the high hill on our left.

"That's our outpost. All the rest is in enemy hands." He paused for a moment and looked at me. "Any more questions?"

"No." My voice was almost inaudible. We went back to the waiting unit. Sasson met us. He was on his feet already, urging the boys to get up. "Everything OK?" he asked.

"Yes," I replied. "We're moving right away."

I gestured to the soldiers to come closer. "You'll dig yourselves in. That's very important. Tomorrow morning they're going to shell us. Get it?" They nodded to show they understood, just the way I'd nodded to the company commander. "Our orders are to hold the outpost at any price." They nodded again. "Well, if you've all got that, we can go!"

"Shalom," Yisrael said, turning to go. He paused for a moment and added: "The pumping station is going to be the depot for any wounded. Hope it won't be needed . . . Good luck!"

He waved goodbye and strode down the slope back to his base. We turned the other way—toward the top of the hill, the highest point.

A stone outpost surrounded by a low fence caught my eye. I halted the unit for a moment. "Let's leave the grenades here," I suggested. "Seems quite safe."

Yosef and Hayim put the heavy bag down gingerly on the lip of the outpost. "Each of you take four or five grenades along." The men took the grenades and hung them on their belts.

"I'll take a few extra," Sasson said. "Can't do any harm."

"Nonsense," Benny sneered. "The less you have to carry, the better." They all laughed.

"Better get ready for a big attack in the morning," I warned them again. "Then these grenades will come in useful."

"Anyone want any more?" asked Hayim. No response.

"OK, give me another few," I said in a demonstrative way.

Hayim handed me two more grenades and then took the bag and placed it on the floor of the dugout. The sack remained leaning against the stone wall.

"We'll leave them here in reserve," I told the others. We continued moving along to the summit of the hill. The place with the low willow trees looked like a suitable location. "Let's put the machine gun there." I called to Sasson. "Seems a good place. It's hidden, and it overlooks the surroundings."

"Not bad." He looked around, sizing it up. "We'll have to collect some stones and dig ourselves in. I'll take Hayim and Gershon with me."

"Right," I agreed. "The others will dig foxholes to your left." Sasson took the machine gun and went off with the other two. The rest of the boys moved off to the left flank of the hill.

"Three of you dig here." I pointed to the spot. "And the other three here, on the further side."

"Maybe the three of us can do it?" Eliahu suggested. "Shabtai, Benny, and I. We want to be together."

"That's right, we want to be together," Shabtai confirmed.

"Alright. I don't mind." The three of them hurried off to their place. "And dig yourselves in well."

I collected Eliezer and Yosef and turned to the position farthest to the left.

"It's hard," Eliezer complained. "Too rocky to dig up."

"Maybe we can pile up stones?" Yosef suggested.

"Come on, dig. Don't be so lazy," I tried to spur them on.

"I'm finished," Eliezer complained. "Let's have a little rest."

I forgot about them for a moment and crawled to the other positions. Morning was approaching. The dark skies became gray and then faint blue. The darkness gave way to the pale light of dawn. I glanced at the slope, which trailed away in a gradual drop, like stone steps, into the thick pine forest at the bottom of the valley. On the right was a hill planted with dense pine trees. There was no movement on it. Beyond the neighboring hills rose a high ridge of hills, which closed all the other hills in like an iron hoof. A white vapor that floated over its slopes gave it an angry sort of splendor, like an awakening volcano whose stones spit fire. I pricked up my ears, trying to catch the sound of any movement in the area. A sleepy quiet hung in the air. *When is it going to start?* I wondered, with a restless anticipation.

The echo of dull, muffled steps broke the silence. The sound of hobnailed boots crunching stones. A voice that grew louder, became sharper. Two bent crouching shapes moved slowly, flexibly, as if walking on tiptoe, their heads dodging to both sides. They held their rifles close to the ground. The way they walked reminded me of a monkey's lope. The two of them climbed up the slope of the hill, coming closer and closer to the summit. They appeared and then vanished every now and then between the rocks and the thorn bushes.

"Trackers," I whispered to Eliezer, who came up to me. I pressed his hand as a sign that he should keep quiet.

"Let's give them a chance to come closer, and then we'll polish them off," he suggested.

"Let's wait and see what's behind them," I whispered. "Get to Sasson as quietly as you can and tell him."

Eliezer slipped away from me and crawled between the rocks toward Sasson's position. Meanwhile the trackers disappeared again. They had taken the direction of the ridge's right side, facing Sasson. The echo of their footsteps still reached me, and I could almost pinpoint their exact location. Soon Eliezer came back.

"It's alright," he whispered hoarsely. "Where are they?"

"Behind the rocks. Over there." He lifted his head carefully to where I'd pointed.

"Here they are!" I exclaimed. The two trackers emerged from the willow trees, about fifty meters from Sasson's position. They halted their bent-over walk for a moment, and stretched themselves to their full height. They looked tall, strong, and vigorous. Their faces were swarthy. I aimed the gun at them instinctively.

A guttural cry from the valley . . . One of them lifted his hand and shouted something loudly. Had he noticed something? Seen someone? Maybe we'd left something lying about on the ground and it had told his sharp eyes where we were. He pulled his mate's arm and dragged him down to the ground with him.

They'd seen us!

I aimed my rifle and tried to catch them before they slipped behind the rocks. But I wasn't quick enough. Shots. Sasson's machine gun. My eyes caught a glimpse of one of them. He sprang into the air and fell on the dense branches of one of the bushes.

"They've spotted us," I cried out.

Eliezer gave me a look of surprise with his black eyes. "One of them has been hit," he said quietly. "Maybe I should crawl there and see what's happened to the other one?"

"No," I said firmly. "I'll do that." He continued looking at me strangely, but said nothing.

I crawled toward the bush, surveying the rocks and bushes carefully. A rifle with a smashed butt lay on the ground, where it had been flung by the soldier whose body lay flat on the bush. Its position seemed strange. He lay on his back on top of the branches, while his face looked downward. His neck was shattered as if it had been twisted around with a pincer. From his wide-open mouth a thin trickle of blood dripped onto the ground, forming a small pool. The sight made me think of a chicken with its neck slit.

I turned my eyes away from him, looking for his mate. While doing so I crawled to the rocks behind the tree. Stains of fresh blood guided me in the direction the other man had taken when he retreated. He had definitely been wounded. His abandoned rifle lay on the ground. My immediate reaction was to aim my gun at the rifle, but I saw at once that its owner had gone. I felt happy. The rifle was a priceless spoil of war. I picked it up.

Thunder, the sound of the heavens crashing on my head, crushing me to the ground. A terrifying, murderous hail of machine guns chattered in my ears. I lay on my face, my strength evaporating in the sweat that poured from every pore of my body. But I couldn't move. All around me flew chips of stone. Clouds of dust lifted into the air. A growing hail of shells pulverized the earth. I felt as if the ground around me was disintegrating, throwing me off it, shedding me. And then everything suddenly fell silent. Time seemed to have gone by endlessly. How long had the whole thing taken? A strange, ominous silence, and a faint ringing in my ears. I crawled close to the outpost I had left earlier.

"Eliezer . . . Yosef," I called softly. No one answered. The ringing in my ears grew stronger.

"Eliezer . . . Yosef . . . Where are you?" I shouted, with a growing feeling of apprehension making my heart beat faster. No reply. I threw myself forward in a mad despair. My hand, sliding over the ground, stopped suddenly and froze on its place. I lowered my eyes to the ground, and they opened wide in terror. My hand was sunk in a trickle of thick, dark blood that wound like a purple thread between the cracks in the rocky soil.

"Eliezer . . . Yosef . . . !" I screamed, but my voice betrayed me: it choked off in my throat, which was torn by my hard breathing.

"See what I've brought," I called out again, brandishing my loot—the enemy soldier's rifle. "I took it from up there," I added. Drops of blood fell from my filthy hands and dripped to the ground. "Why don't you answer me?" I begged them. When no answer came, my hands lost their grip, and the rifle rolled into the pools of blood that ran down the slope. I looked down and fixed my eyes on the piece of ground in front of me. Thousands of black cracks stood before me, as if myriads of hidden roots had emerged from under the rocks and were cutting up and overturning the layer of earth that covered the ground. The crevices were red. Blood trickled into them. I rose from my place, in horror, fleeing from the earth's open maw. Blood . . . blood . . . Shock flushed my face. Lava boiled in my blood. Rifle shots echoed in my head. Blood . . . I crawled crazily over the blood-stained stones lying next to the lip of the dugout. Eliezer and Yosef were lying on their bellies, with their backs to the sky. Their destroyed heads, which rested on the stones of the dugout lip, had become a mixture of shattered bones, hair, and flesh dripping blood. I came up close to them and turned them over onto their backs, with a secret hope. Nothing was left of their faces as I remembered them.

My hands clung to the damp earth in despair. I felt I was wallowing in the warm red mud that lay all around them.

"Boys," I wailed, "what happened to you?" Tears flowed out of my eyes.

I lay there crying bitterly, clutching the earth, holding it tight, until a fresh commotion aroused me from this senseless torpor. The thunder of shots, the shouts of people, and the shrieking of whistles . . . The enemy was coming nearer. They were jubilant. They felt triumphant. I peered over the lip of the dugout, and waited. Two rows of soldiers emerged from the wood in the valley. They scampered toward the top of the hill.

Where was the rifle? I looked around me fearfully. Once more I stared at my mates' smashed heads. Where was the rifle? . . . It had fallen out of my hands. Maybe on the edge of the dugout. I forced myself to crawl there. Sure enough, the rifle was lying there. I pulled it toward me. It felt heavy, hard, and clumsy. It slipped between my wet fingers and fell onto the flat stones. I caught hold of it again and tried to pull it toward me. This time I held it more firmly. I wiped the blood from my hands onto my trousers.

The enemy's cries came closer, crowding the hollow space of the valley. Now my hand was on the rifle. I aimed it at the figures moving on the slope, and got them in the sights. My arms were shaking. I pressed the butt against my shoulder with all my strength. But my hands shook, and my whole body trembled, down to my knees. I couldn't even aim the rifle straight. Strong shots from Sasson's machine gun stopped my shuddering, and at the same time I heard the loud bellows of the enemy advancing toward me. The rifle was in my hand, its sight set on the line of soldiers. A man appeared plumb in the center of the sight. I fired with anger and despair.

I reloaded the rifle and fired over and over again. They came closer. Some of them fell to the ground, and others remained standing. Now there were only fifty meters between us.

How many of them were there? The slope was full of them. I fired and fired, but it didn't help. Cries. Their distorted faces moved from side to side. The shots rang out, everything was rocking about, my senses were becoming blurred. I fired and fired. I stretched my hand out suddenly to the hand grenade in my belt. I took the pin out. Four seconds to wait. They were coming closer. I threw the grenade at them. It exploded with a clap like thunder. Splinters hissed and shrieked all around me. The sound of machine gun bullets chattered in my ears again. I threw another grenade at them. More machine gun bullets. I threw another grenade. The air became thicker and hotter. The dense smell of gunpowder, the cries of the wounded men, the shrill whistles, the noisy, heavy drumming of soldiers attacking.

And then, suddenly, the noise died down and everything went silent. It seemed as if all sound had sank and buried itself in the earth. The enemy soldiers vanished behind the stones. The last attackers returned at a run to the edge of the wood.

The attack had been repulsed!

"Are you alright?" Sasson's voice echoed in my ears. It sounded very far away.

Should I tell him the truth? They were going to attack us again. I would tell him later. When it was all over.

"Yes," I replied, my voice trembling. "And what about you?"

"Hayim's been wounded," I heard a muffled voice. Eliahu was crawling up to the dugout. I heard him moving on my left.

"Stop!" I called out. He stopped behind a nearby rock. I didn't want him to see the dead men, and so I crawled toward him so that I could meet him halfway.

"He got away," he mumbled. I looked up at him. Tense eyes, a hard, cruel look. He was breathing heavily and sweating.

"Who got away?"

"That dirty bastard Benny."

"What about Shabtai?"

"Dead. Put his head out and got one right in the forehead."

"How could you let Benny get away like that?" I shouted angrily.

"When Shabtai got killed, Benny started shouting that we'd come to the wrong hill. 'It's all a mistake, a mistake,' he screamed. 'This hill's too low. We're finished . . . If we don't retreat, we'll all be killed.'"

"So what did you do?"

"I yelled at him and tried to calm him down. But he was half crazy. Threw his gun on the ground. 'Pick it up!' I told him."

"You mean to say you let him throw his rifle on the ground?" I accused him.

"He said his fingers were sweating. I was angry, and I hit him on the shoulder with the butt of my rifle. He started shouting that I'd wounded him. Then he began sprinting toward the rocks. I called him to come back. But he buggered off, the coward. Told me he was going to crawl to the first-aid station."

"I hope the shit gets killed on the way!" I was so angry I could hardly breathe.

"What about the others?" Eliahu threw a glance at the dugout.

"Everything's OK," I lied. "We're getting ready for another attack." He didn't look convinced. "Go back to your post and tell them to get ready," I ordered in a firm voice. He shuffled his foot and then said: "Maybe I can join Hayim and Yosef?"

"No," I said. "You've got to go back to your own dugout."

"Maybe we're really on the wrong hill?" he asked hesitantly. "The scout who brought us here could have made a mistake."

But when he saw my angry look, he stopped talking and changed the subject: "You've got blood on you. Been wounded?"

"Just a splinter," I tried to sound casual. "Nothing much."

"But your whole shirt is filthy with blood. And your hands also . . . Sure you're alright?" he went on with growing suspicion.

"Nonsense. Nothing to worry about. Crawl over to Sasson's outpost," I added, without insisting that he should return to his former dugout. "Tell Sasson I said you can join them."

"Sure you're not hurt?" His mind wasn't at rest, I could see that.

"Yes, of course," I rapped impatiently. "Go on, crawl to Sasson. We haven't got much time. The attack will start again soon."

Eliahu looked at me as if he wanted to hear something encouraging. Then he said, "As you like," in a flat tone, and crawled off to Sasson's position.

I stared ahead of me, to the chain of hills on the horizon. *Something's going on there,* I said to myself. *Something's going on.* I took hold of the field glasses that hung around my neck: Ilan's field glasses. They were dusty and battered.

Wearily I lifted the field glasses to my eyes.

CHAPTER 12

A FADING TWILIGHT

Thirst. Pain. Shattered, creaking bones. Fire burning inside me, consuming all my strength. "Water! Water!" I tried to shout. But the words were swallowed up. A murky whirlpool of smoke curled and spun around in front of my eyes. Acrid smoke blocked my breathing, stinging my lips, almost choking me. "Water! Water!" I spat in despair. "Water!" a shattered groan burst from my dry mouth.

A wet, searing heat blazed in my mouth. A red-hot fire ate at my innards. A clear, blinding fire lit up suddenly. Fire . . . flame . . . Dry, discordant whistles pierced my ears. An iron saw creaked over my bones, cutting deep and scattering splinters all around, sawing mercilessly.

Smoke covered my eyes once more, heavy, sulfurous smoke, salty and thick. "Water! Water!"

Everything in front of me was blurred. A dense darkness enveloped my eyes. Voices and other sounds filtered through this pitch-black curtain: people running, the sound of frantic breathing, the thunderous roar of guns, the sound of iron scraping and setting my teeth on edge. Suddenly consciousness returned to me. Thousands of bottles of cool, clear water surrounded me.

I grabbed the bottles and drank out of them, drank quickly, greedily, gurgling and slurping, with lust and insanity. A hollow, strident bubbling sound came from the mouths of the bottles as I dashed their contents down. *Plop . . . plop,* the water bubbled. But my thirst wasn't quenched. It grew worse, more violent, until it nearly drove me crazy. I grabbed another bottle, and another. *Plop, plop, plop.* "Drink, drink! Water!" I croaked. "Water!"

Plop . . . plop . . . plop. A bubbling sound that grew louder, a pump that beat strongly. I ran over the smoke-covered hills in a frenzy, holding bottles of water. Ran until I was breathless and floated on plains covered with low, leaden skies. My hands were stretched out to heaven, and my fingers were clenched in a plea: "Water, water!" I wailed. Burning flames ran wild inside me, boiling lead was poured into my body, my insides ached and screamed out loud, my whole body writhed in agony. A giant gun was drying everything out, and I ran around doubled-up with pain. A heavy, suffocating smoke arose from the soil, as if thousands of huge bonfires had been lit around me with wet branches, which gave off damp steam. I tried to break through to the fire, crawling and winding between the glowing embers. Between the damp branches. I picked them up in my hand and licked them with my tongue: "Water, water, water!" But I swallowed only fire and embers. Only flames.

The pump beat again, strongly and without mercy, until my shattered bones creaked with pain. Thick smoke covered the rocks, like the smoke of a steam engine. A hot breeze blew and caught fire. The sound of shots came to my ears. A cruel, stabbing explosion accompanied by cries and the sobbing of wounded men. My comrades had all been killed, and I was left alone. The snarl of battle had died down, the day was dwindling, the sun was about to set, the skies were turning the color of charcoal, the rocks were frozen. Soon I would feel nothing. I'd sink . . . sink into a whirlpool . . . A circle of smoke curled in front me, going around and expanding, going around and opening up. I was sinking into a black cave, sliding and slipping over a muddy path. Faded lines of light dancing up and down. Abyss. Darkness. Blackness.

The trumpet cheered again. Sizzling sounds, the hoarse yelps of dogs. Something hammered at me, hitting hard. The sound of drums rising. The rattle of train wheels rushing by, the creaking of iron wheels being stopped suddenly: a mighty, thunderous waterfall. The reverberation of an explosion of rocks hammered my head. Hammered it with a mighty wind, a storm.

I was sinking. The black circles went on spreading, expanding, opening a dark maw, to swallow, to sweep away. I wanted to stretch my hand out to the sides, to hold onto something. But everything was hollow, empty. I couldn't hold anything tightly. Like those bows in the heavens, that I had tried to grasp a long time ago. Bows . . .

Everything was uprooted from me: the pain, the thirst, and the fire . . . A dull, cracked sliver of light still danced about, but it was dying away, fading and growing dimmer. The flicker of a faint thought, which was vague, cloudy, hurt, and battered between blank, vacant walls . . . To return . . . to return . . . I was drowning, diving, diving deep down. Sleep . . . slumber . . . a paralyzing slumber. A warm stream poured inside me and rose. I was dragged into an infinite vacuum, into a blank chasm that was mummified, fossilized, and I could do nothing, nothing at all . . .

Weariness . . . slumber . . . drums . . . darkness . . .